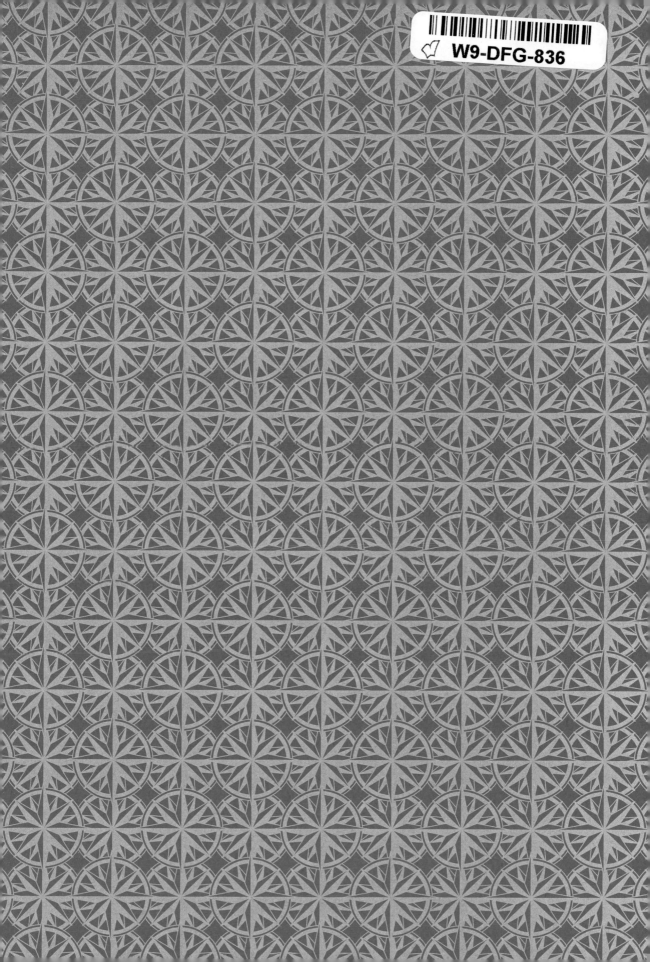

WINTER QUIET ENFOLDS EL CAPITAN AND THE MERCED RIVER AT SUNSET.

YOSEMITE

An American Treasure

By Kenneth Brower

Prepared by the Special Publications Division
National Geographic Society, Washington, D.C.

PRECEDING PAGES: BRIDALVEIL FALL TUMBLES 620 FEET. ABOVE: UPPER YOSEMITE FALL THUNDERS PAST A SUMMER VISITOR.

"*B*ut no temple made with hands can compare with Yosemite. Every rock in its walls seems to glow with life. . . . as if into this one mountain mansion Nature had gathered her choicest treasures. . . ." —*John Muir*

Yosemite:
An American Treasure
By Kenneth Brower

Published by
The National Geographic
Society

Gilbert M. Grosvenor
*President and
Chairman of the Board*

Melvin M. Payne
Thomas W. McKnew
Chairmen Emeritus

Owen R. Anderson
Executive Vice President

Robert L. Breeden
*Senior Vice President,
Publications and
Educational Media*

Prepared by
The Special Publications
Division

Donald J. Crump
Director

Philip B. Silcott
Associate Director

Bonnie S. Lawrence
Assistant Director

Staff for this book

Toni Eugene
Managing Editor

Charles E. Herron
Illustrations Editor

Marianne Koszorus
Art Director

Alice Jablonsky
Senior Researcher

Kim Kostyal
Researcher

Martha C. Christian
Consulting Editor

Richard M. Crum
H. Robert Morrison
Thomas J. O'Neill
Cynthia Russ Ramsay
Gene S. Stuart
Picture Legend Writers

Susan I. Friedman
Joseph F. Ochlak
Map Research

Sandra F. Lotterman
Editorial Assistant

Artemis S. Lampathakis
Illustrations Assistant

*Engraving, Printing, and
Product Manufacture*

George V. White
Director

Vincent P. Ryan
*Manager, Manufacturing
and Quality Management*

David V. Showers
Production Manager

Kevin P. Heubusch
*Production Project
Manager*

Lewis R. Bassford
Timothy H. Ewing
Assistant Production Managers

Carol R. Curtis
Marisa J. Farabelli
Karen Katz
Lisa A. LaFuria
Dru M. Stancampiano
Marilyn J. Williams
Staff Assistants

Michael G. Young
Indexer

RIGHT: PINE NEEDLES AND AUTUMN
LEAVES FLOAT ON FERN SPRING.

CLIMBERS SCALE THE SHEER NORTHWEST FACE OF HALF DOME.

Contents

My Yosemite

A Prologue

"Yosemite" derives from the Miwok word for the Indians who lived in the valley—the *yo'hem-iteh*. It has nothing to do with any Old World tongue, but as a small boy trying to make sense of language I forced English meaning into it. I heard it as "Yoursemite." When asked if I wanted to go to Yosemite, I would answer, "Yes! Let's go to Mysemite." I thought the place was mine.

Early in my ownership, at the age of two, I got lost on the floor of my valley. Following some butterfly, some scent, some proprietary urge, I wandered away from our cabin at Yosemite Lodge. My mother thought I was with my father. My father thought the reverse. For an hour or two I explored the valley on my own. My parents are vague about the length of time; for them, clearly, it was an eternity. Black bears and coyotes roam the valley floor. Bucks browse there, sharp horned, temperamental.

"Have you checked down by the river?" the chambermaid asked, her voice hoarse and funereal.

———————————

Last light gilds Horsetail Fall's thousand-foot cascade from the summit of El Capitan. Yosemite lures hikers and mountaineers with rugged upland grandeur softened by meadows, forests, lakes, and fast-flowing waters.

"Have you checked down by the river?" The question seems to have burned itself into my mother's memory.

But I wasn't drowned in the river, or eaten by bears. I wasn't discovered in the bulrushes on the banks of the Merced. I showed up at the valley gas station and returned to my parents in the company of the woman who had found me. I was cheerful, by all accounts. Whatever I had been up to that morning, it seems to have agreed with me.

My family's history and Yosemite's are all intertwined. My maternal great-grandfather, John P. Irish, was a commissioner of Yosemite. He favored state control of the park. He was ex officio and philosophically the archenemy of John Muir, principal advocate of federal control and a *national* park. My great-grandfather was not quite the villain Muir imagined him to be, and vice versa. In retrospect, both men appear to have been equally enlightened about Yosemite.

The commissioner's daughter, my grandmother Frankie, remembered four-day trips by stagecoach to the valley from Oakland. My mother recalls Frankie's description of the dust from the stages—terrible, filling the valley in those days. She also remembers dinner table talk about Muir. "That old nature-faker," my great-grandfather used to say.

In 1918, when my father was six, he made his first trip to Yosemite, a three-day odyssey from Berkeley in a 1916 Maxwell. He liked Yosemite but discovered in himself a fear of heights. When the family set off up the steep trail to Sentinel Dome, he stayed behind. Later, at the bridge below Vernal Fall—in those days just a log with a handrail—he refused to cross.

The Brower family kept returning to the mountains. My father's fear underwent a peculiar transmutation: He challenged it, and it reversed itself. He became a rock-climber, and the fear became fear's opposite. He spent much of his youth—most of the 1930s—on sheer faces in Yosemite and elsewhere in the High Sierra. He has a number of first ascents in the valley.

The climbing seemed an end in itself then. Now it is clear that it was training for what would become his lifework. Like John Muir, my father would spend his youth as a mountaineer and his maturity as a preservationist. He became the first executive director of Muir's Sierra Club. As Muir had done before him, he redefined the American conservation movement.

My mother, granddaughter of Muir's old nemesis, married David Brower, the man many considered to be Muir reincarnate.

I often find myself wondering about my escape into the valley—about those hours I was missing at the age of two. Where did I go? What did I see and do? I remember nothing at all of it.

There are home movies of that trip, and I have searched the footage for clues. The film has shifted yellow after 42 years, but that has failed to dim entirely the green of the Yosemite meadows, the albedo of the granite walls. My mother, slim and young, holds me on her hip and introduces me to an eight-point stag. Both the stag and my mother are a little nervous and tentative. I can make no connection with that little boy. Nothing about him sparks any associations. He looks, if you want my opinion, a bit dim and strange about the eyes.

In walks about the valley, I have tried to reconstruct those missing hours. The smell was the fragrance of incense cedar and alder. The sound was the sound of water—the roar of Yosemite Falls, if my escape took me in one direction; the slow, whispery currents and eddies of the Merced, if I walked in the other. In the foreground were tall trees in shadow—ponderosa pine and incense cedar—and beyond, in sunlight, the white-granite sheerness of Yosemite walls, so bright they were almost painful. The Sierra Nevada, said Muir, was "The Range of Light." The valley lies at the center of that luminous range. Its walls are like light crystallized, then fractured and sculpted and exfoliated.

Last December I stopped my car in the valley to watch a coyote hunting in a snowy meadow. A boy and his mother had stopped their bikes and stood astride them, studying the coyote. There was an edge to the air, and their two breaths were condensing above them. The coyote was wolfing something down—the tail of a squirrel, maybe, though it seemed a trifle small for that. The tail gone, the coyote resumed its hunting. It walked forward stealthily, head low. It stopped, swung its nose slightly from side to side, casting about for a scent, then held still and stared straight ahead. Its breath condensed above it—one puff, then another. It pounced. Landing stiff legged on its front feet, it broke through the thin crust of snow. For a moment it paused, then poked its nose into the hole it had made. I tried to see this coyote as the boy on the bike must see it. He was a stand-in for that other boy of many years ago.

I have a suspicion that my disappearance in Yosemite, if I could somehow recall it, would prove to be a key to me. The best times of my life have been in wild places. I am a writer whose books and articles are always set outdoors. My stories, I have learned finally, must have a bit of outside in them or they never come alive. I never really *feel* a piece of country until I am alone in it. The moment I put a hill, or a gully, or a few turns of the trail between myself and my companions, the world is illuminated, as if some hand had thrown a switch.

Perhaps the switch was thrown first on the day I was lost and alone in Yosemite. My parents lost track of time while I was missing; perhaps it was the same for me. Maybe the hours passed like days.

Why lately do I find myself so often on the bridge beneath Yosemite Falls? How is it that the thunder of the cataract speaks to me so? Yosemite Falls speaks to everyone, of course. The cataract has a sphere of influence; its tons of falling water generate a climate and a wind of their own. A quarter mile from the bridge, the temperature drops abruptly, and walkers button their jackets against a sudden cool breeze. Sometimes, buttoning my own, I am nearly certain that my escape took me this way. Standing on the bridge, in the roar and fast-scudding mist, I find myself smiling and wondering.

At the other end of Yosemite Falls, 2,500 feet above the bridge, John Muir once inched down to where Yosemite Creek jets outward from the cliff. "I concluded not to attempt to go nearer," he says, "but, nevertheless, against reasonable judgment, I did." Muir stuffed some artemisia leaves into his mouth, hoping the bitter taste would work against vertigo. "I . . . got my heels well set, and worked sidewise twenty or thirty feet to a point close to the out-plunging current. Here the view is perfectly free down into the heart of the bright irised throng of comet-like streamers into which the whole ponderous volume of the fall separates, two or three hundred feet below the brow."

Then again, maybe I didn't escape toward the falls at all. When one is two years old and on his own, a waterfall is not necessary. On the day of my disappearance, perhaps I got a rush like Muir's in just standing beside some brook.

Muir won the battle over Yosemite, and my great-grandfather lost. In 1890, Yosemite became a national park, a reserve for all Americans. In 1984 it became a World Heritage Site—and the incense of its cedars, the monumental grandeur of its walls, the irised streamers of its falls became the domain of all the peoples of the world. My little childhood misunderstanding, "Mysemite," amused the adults who heard it, but I was entirely correct, of course. It *is* Mysemite—and it is Yoursemite, too.

Yosemite National Park includes nearly 1,200 square miles of western Sierra Nevada natural wonder—an area about the size of Rhode Island. More than 450 miles of roads lead 3.5 million visitors each year through Yosemite's scenic splendor. Hiking trails totaling 800 miles lace the backcountry, which makes up 94 percent of the park. FOLLOWING PAGES: Powers of nature sculpted mountains and valleys from masses of granite. Names given to some features—cathedral, dome, tower, and arch—reflect admiration for structures fashioned by human craftsmen.

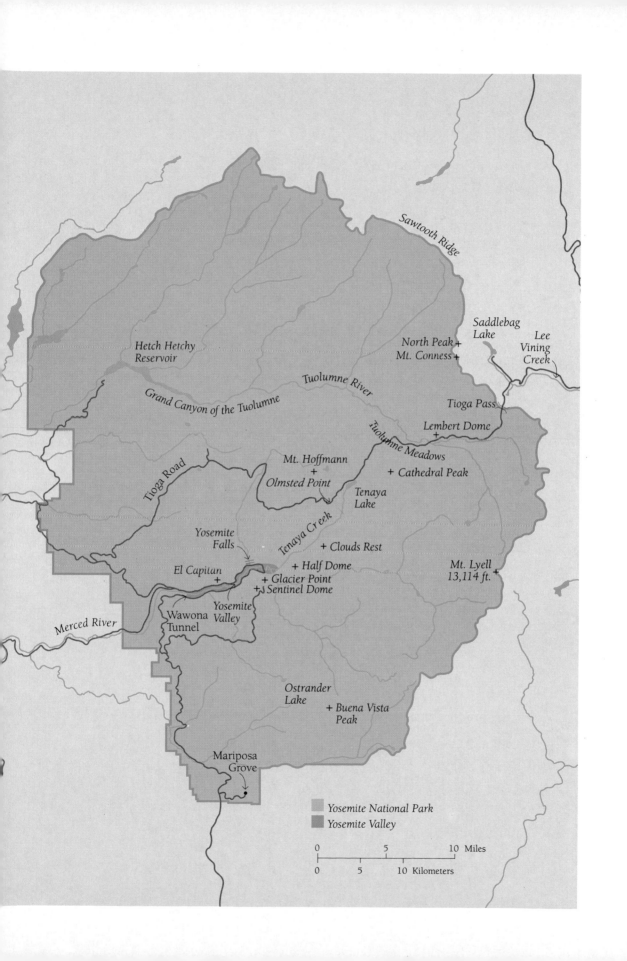

Sawtooth Ridge

Saddlebag
Lake

Lee
Vining
Creek

North Peak +
Mt. Conness +

Hetch Hetchy
Reservoir

Tuolumne River

Tioga Pass

Grand Canyon of the Tuolumne

Lembert Dome +

Tuolumne Meadows

Mt. Hoffmann
+
Olmsted Point

+ Cathedral Peak

Tioga Road

Tenaya
Lake

Tenaya Creek

Yosemite
Falls

+ Clouds Rest

El Capitan

+ Half Dome
+ Glacier Point
+ Sentinel Dome

Mt. Lyell
13,114 ft. +

Wawona
Tunnel

Yosemite
Valley

Merced River

Ostrander
Lake

+ Buena Vista
Peak

Mariposa
Grove

Yosemite National Park
Yosemite Valley

0   5   10 Miles

0   5   10 Kilometers

Clouds Rest

Mt. Lyell

Half Dome

Nevada Fall

Glacier Point

Vernal Fall

Cathedral
Rocks

Fire and Ice

*T*wenty-five million years ago, the Sierra Nevada had just begun its upwarp. The great range was only great-to-be. It would be named by the Spanish, millions of years later, for its jagged skyline of peaks, so like a saw, *sierra,* and for its snows, *nevada,* but for now it was neither snowy nor sawlike. The central section of the Sierra was a single massive block of the earth's crust tilted toward the southwest. The tilt at first was slight, just enough to accelerate the streams. The streams, hastening, etched valleys.

Fifteen million years ago, the greatest of those valleys was still just an incipience. Its floor was broad and open. Its stream took wide, lazy meanders through a landscape of gentle curves. The bordering hills stood perhaps 500 to 1,000 feet tall and were forested with hardwoods — maple, willow, sycamore. It was a country fragrant of magnolia, pungent of laurel. Tapirs, rhinos, piglike deer, bear-dogs, mastodons, and beavers browsed or rooted or hunted in the forest. In the upper valley, on the prominence that *(Continued on page 24)*

Sunset warms the weathered face of El Capitan in Yosemite. Millions of years ago, magma heated by earth's internal fires built up masses of granite in Yosemite; erosion exposed the rock; water and ice carved it.

Rancheria Creek plunges toward Hetch Hetchy Reservoir, north of Yosemite Valley (above). Water began sculpting the region, cutting deep V-shaped ravines. Icicles in a stream bed (opposite) recall the rivers of ice that gouged Yosemite Valley wider and deeper into its present U shape. FOLLOWING PAGES: *Soft snow dusts the park. From El Capitan to the silver wisp of Bridalveil Fall, the U curve of the valley reflects glacial scouring.*

would be called Clouds Rest, low cliffs of pale rock caught the light. A batholith, a huge subterranean mass built up by molten rock within the earth, had been exposed there; a hint of things to come. But Clouds Rest as yet lacked the elevation to gather clouds and make them comfortable.

The batholith was composed of masses of rock that marked separate invasions of magma. The rock was granite, composed chiefly of feldspar and quartz. Varying proportions of each mineral determined the species of granite. Texture determined the subspecies—whether El Capitan granite, with its salt-and-pepper look; or Cathedral Peak granodiorite, with its huge, pale crystals scattered like bits of paper windblown against a gray sky.

*T*he rock was hard and durable and took a fine polish. It would have made good material for sculpture, except that it lay too deep to be worked. The forms in it were all unrealized, like the "David" before Michelangelo freed it from the marble. The 3,500-foot megalith that would become El Capitan was just a rounded summit, its white granite covered with sedimentary rock and forest. The great monuments to be called Basket Dome, Sentinel Dome, North Dome were all imprisoned in the same matrix of sedimentary rock. The pinnacle of Leaning Tower was not yet a pinnacle and did not yet lean. It was "Little Knob," if it was anything. El Capitan was not even "Corporal."

There is a lesson, in retrospect, in that old, unprepossessing landscape. It has to do with the enormous potential dormant in any terrain. The valley was no more spectacular, on the face of it, than your grandfather's back forty or your uncle's place upstate, yet chasms waited in it, soaring megaliths, dizzying white verticalities of stone. Latent in the slow meanders of the streams were waterfalls, all thunder and exuberance and windblown mist.

The valley's eternal hills were not eternal at all. They were fleeting. The rounded forms there were scarcely more permanent than forms in the clouds.

There was no human intellect on hand to intuit the lesson. *Merychippus,* the first of the hypsodont or long-toothed horses, may have wandered up into the valley from the plain to the west. It grew no larger than a newborn colt and ran on three-toed feet, yet a horse trader from the future, on checking the teeth, would have found it familiar. The high-crowned teeth were an adaptation to the blades and stems of abrasive grasses that had recently taken over the plains. The little animal was large brained for an ancestral horse, but geological speculation was beyond it.

Prosynthetoceras, a strange antelope-like creature with its horns on its nose, may have ventured into the highlands and mixed with the resident tapirs, rhinos, bear-dogs, and mastodons. The animals wandered the landscape; they were unequipped to ponder it. It would take many millennia of human history, indeed, before life grasped the infinities of geological time that are its prerequisite and its context. The illuminations of the geologists Lyell and Hutton and William "Strata" Smith lay in the far-distant future. When the valley began, the ancestors of John Muir, who would be its great explainer, were hunched on some African savanna, digging tubers and contemplating the flowers.

For millions of years the block of the Sierra slowly rose. The increased tilt of the block again accelerated the stream, and by five million years ago the valley was cut perhaps 800 feet deeper. The walls grew much more rugged. Streams cut through the steepening hills, sending tributary creeks cascading down to join the main one. El Capitan had formed a distinct brow. Its face was wooded still, but granite crags and pinnacles were beginning to stand out among the trees. The hardwood forests gave way to conifers. Redwoods and their relatives then dominated the forests of the Northern Hemisphere. *Metasequoia,* the dawn redwood, a deciduous conifer, grew in widely scattered pockets of the west, as did the ancestor of the giant sequoia of today, a more conventional conifer, evergreen, and the biggest thing that has ever lived.

If any ancestral horse wandered up now from the plain, it was likely *Pliohippus,* the first of the one-toed horses. *Pliohippus* came on hooves as we know them. It was an animal large enough that the time-traveling horse trader might have saddled up and ridden.

It was during this period that a new land bridge from South America allowed porcupines, giant ground sloths, armadillos, and glyptodonts to wander north. (The glyptodont was a giant armadillo-like creature, armored like a tank, one species equipped with a heavy, spiny mace at the tip of the tail.) An Ice Age land bridge from Asia brought moose, caribou, bison, bighorn sheep, mammoths, and wolves. These new arrivals mingled with creatures that had evolved in North America: the horses, tapirs, weasels, wolverines, badgers, skunks, camels, mastodons, deer, pronghorns, coyotes.

Some of these first encounters occurred in the valley, perhaps. It would have been an interesting time. The wolf meets the wolverine. The wolf meets the dire wolf, its gigantic North American counterpart. The wolf encounters the porcupine. The porcupine meets the skunk. The mammoth meets the mastodon. The coyote tries to solve the armadillo. The wolverine tries to solve the glyptodont.

By three million years ago, the central Sierra had approached its present elevation. Then the sources of the valley's river were pushed about 3,000 feet higher. The young summits, thrust up into thin, cold air, began to collect heavy snows. The mountains were *nevada* at last, and they were becoming *sierra* as well, losing their roundedness, the peaks growing angular and hollow sided. By two million years ago, the valley's stream had become a mountain torrent and had carved the floor into a canyon perhaps 2,000 feet deep.

*W*inters grew colder. Windblown snow collected on the northerly and easterly sides of the peaks, where wind shadows and sun shadows coincided. The thin, dry air was cool even in summer. The drifted snow failed to melt in the warm months; winters added new snow on top of the old; the snow compacted to ice; the ice became glaciers. From those first small fields of ice—blue-white seeds strewn on the shadowy sides of the peaks—an ice age blossomed. The glaciers in these mountains were never part of the continental ice sheet that covered Canada and much of the northeastern and midwestern United States. The glaciation never buried the peaks under an ice sheet, as the peaks of Greenland or Antarctica are buried today. The higher Sierra peaks made rocky islands—nunataks—above a frozen sea. But if never quite an ocean, the glacial sea was mighty. The ice mantle was vaster here than on any North American range of the same latitude.

Life retreated from the range. The giant sequoias, immune to time but not to cold, died where they stood. Firs, spruces, pines ceased to germinate. Over time the resinous scent of conifers gave way to the raw scentlessness of glacier. Aspens, alders, and other deciduous trees surrendered their leaves a final time and never tried again. Willows perished alongside frozen streams. The good, ascorbic aroma of willows in spring departed the mountains. No more willows; no more spring. A few animals—the rhinos, the bear-dogs, the piglike deer— had not survived to see the ice arrive. The others withdrew to lower elevations. *Felis atrox,* the atrocious lion; *Smilodon,* the saber-toothed cat; and the dire wolf all left off their hunting in the high country and confined themselves to the warmth of the plains. Their successors-to-be, the mountain lion and the wolf, did the same, as did the badger, the weasel, and the skunk. A few eccentric individuals probably chose to stay. Idiosyncrasy and stubbornness seem not just human traits. The cold turned them into monuments, like the carcasses of those seals that wander inland to die in the dry valleys of Antarctica.

Where life, in the form of sequoias, had once towered 300 feet above earth, life now lay low. Studying modern glaciers, we can guess at what this reign of ice and snow must have been like. Older, simple forms survived once again and carried on. Pink snow algae colonized melt depressions in the snow, pocking old snowbanks with circles of dilute red. The pink depressions might have been the giant paw prints of the atrocious lion after a kill—except, of course, that the lion had departed. On the bare rock of the nunataks, lichens grew in their whorls and circles. The lichens might have been abstractions by aboriginal rock painters, except that aborigines had yet to arrive. The lichens made the thinnest living veneer; a scaly paint, as on old masterpieces, yet in pigments strong—virulent orange, yellow-green, sulfur yellow.

Ice worms inhabited glaciers and perennial snowbanks. Fog and clouds now shrouded the mountains, but when the sun broke through, the worms emerged. They were black, and efficiently absorbed the radiance of a stingy sun. They inched and writhed through a glittering landscape of decaying crystals, feeding on snow algae and on debris blown up from unfrozen lands below.

Bears of the ursine sort were gone to lower elevations. (Sleeping through a single winter is one thing; through a glacial age, another.) Insect bears took their place—cave beetles in the dens of their ice grottoes on the glaciers. Rabbits were gone, but the insects called springtails remained. They bent the springs of their elastic caudal stylets under them and hopped about the snow and ice. Glacier fleas and glacier mites foraged for what they could. Nival insects—insects adapted to snow—are wonderfully hardy in the cold, especially those dwelling at high elevations. They can hibernate for prolonged periods at any stage of development. Burrowing into the snow, crawling under a rock or into a crevice, they suspend their animation and survive for years. (This hardiness deserts them at the other end of the thermometer. Glacier fleas and mites are so thoroughly creatures of the cold that the warmth of a human hand can kill them.)

The unearthly howl of the dire wolf—if dire wolves expressed themselves that way—had ceased to echo from the peaks. The cough of the atrocious lion—if those cats coughed, indeed—had ceased to resound in the valleys. There were sounds still—the crack of frost-riven rock, the *whumph* and sibilant rush of avalanche—but those were few and far between, punctuation in a great silence.

In the rivers of ice the granite of the mountains finally met its Michelangelo. Hundreds of feet beneath the tunnels of the ice worms, at the sides and bottoms of the glaciers, ice was sculpting the country. It achieved its large effects by quarrying whole blocks of granite and carrying them away. For every thousand feet of its depth, a glacier generates thirty tons of pressure per square foot on the rock beneath. It is power enough to move mountains.

"What is of all things most yielding/Can overcome that which is most hard. . . ?" the poet Lao Tzu asked, seven millennia ago. The answer he wanted was water. It would have spoiled his paradox, but the poet might have added that water in its cold, unyielding form overcomes hardness best of all.

The great Ice Age lasted about two million years—a blink in the geological history of the valley—but that blink gave the country its distinction. The forms waiting in the granite leaped into being.

Scouring and grinding, the glaciers etched the landscape. The ice wrote its signature everywhere in the high country. Small rocks borne along by the glaciers left striations and grooves on the granite they traveled over. Larger rocks left the single chevrons of percussion marks, the wings pointing upglacier, and crescentic chatter marks, the horns pointing downglacier. Finer materials in suspension buffed the granite until it shone like glass. Streams flowing beneath the ice left tracks of fluted, water-polished rock. Melting ice left huge boulders—glacial erratics—balanced in strange places, precarious and Daliesque. In advance and recession, the glaciers deposited their detritus in the loops of moraines. Excavating granite headwalls, they carved the bowls of steep-walled basins called cirques. Where cirques cut in from opposite sides, they whittled ridges down to the narrow, toothy crests called arêtes. The ice transformed the high country into a sierra indeed.

But if the ice left a masterpiece, it was down in the valley. The valley was invaded several times by trunk glaciers. Tributary rivers of ice flowed down into it, merged, and gouged the V-shaped, meandering river canyon into a U-shaped and only slightly sinuous glacial trough. It pared the craggy walls of the canyon back to sheer granite cliffs. It cut away extraneous detail; nothing remained but the pure and the bold.

The cascading streams, which millions of years before had entered the valley from the sides, had tumbled down intermediate ridges, impatient to get to the valley floor. Now they had lost all patience. The glaciers had cut away all the ledges. The streams now flung themselves headlong into space.

The valley was more beautiful in emergence, perhaps, than it had ever been, or would ever be again. Melting, the glaciers had left lakes. When the tongue of the last glacier's terminus had withdrawn, retreating up the giant, ice-carved staircase at the valley's head, meltwater replaced it, filling the valley floor from wall to wall. Hanging valleys, stranded high on the main walls by the ice, sent lofty waterfalls plunging into a blue, fjord-like lake. The granite cliffs were as yet uncluttered at the base by talus from rockfalls off the oversteepened faces. The clean, Doric architecture of the rock was unsoftened by vegetation. The reflective face of the granite was undimmed by any dark foreground of conifers. But things were a little too stark, perhaps. The valley was all cold stone and chill waters. Glaciers, in their moving of mountains and their excavation of valleys, are curiously like man in the same enterprises. Raw glacial till has a disorderly and unnatural look, like mine tailings or road fill.

Mosses colonized the unsorted till of the terminal moraine. Dryas, with its white and yellow flowers, followed, then pioneer grasses. The valley was never more poignantly beautiful, perhaps, than in this renaissance. (If spring is sweet after four months of winter, then how is spring after thousands of years of it?) Life had returned to the valley. Seasons as we know them had returned. The blades of the pioneer grasses nodded, in their green simplicity, against the Doric simplicity of the stone.

*P*rostrate willows succeeded the grasses. The good, clean aroma of willows in springtime was on the breeze again. Shrubby willows succeeded the prostrate, starting recumbent themselves, then growing erect. Alders succeeded the willows. The lake filled in with sediment and became a meadow. Meadow mice invaded, laying out their labyrinths of runways. Coyotes hunted the mice. They stalked, stopped, bounded high, and landed forefeet together in that stiff-legged coyote pounce. Mule deer grazed the meadow edges. Their elegant heads were forever coming up as they ruminated. The black noses were forever testing the breeze. The great ears were forever rotating to fix on some barely perceptible noise in the distance.

Oaks impinged, constricting the meadow. Ponderosa pines impinged on the oaks, shading out their predecessors. Old ponderosas fell, decayed, and became nurseries for grubs. Black bears raided the nurseries, clawing away dead bark. Grizzlies padded through, and on their appearance the black bears vanished. Water ouzels did their dipping dance in the mist of the waterfalls. Golden eagles wheeled in the valley sky. The valley was its most beautiful right then, maybe, as successional processes reached something like a climax.

Or does beauty require a beholder? Wolves seem to enjoy a view, and mountain lions, but do they bring an aesthetic to it? Is landscape more to them than a place to find deer? A bipedal hunter arrived. The first human, walking through the portal between El Capitan and Cathedral Rocks, discovered Yosemite. The valley was never more beautiful, perhaps, than then.

Clouds swirling about Half Dome suggest a scene from hundreds of thousands of years ago, when rivers of ice buried most of Yosemite. A bank of clouds fills the valley in a view of the monolith from Washburn Point (above). Frost split off blocks of granite at the base of the 4,800-foot-high dome, quarrying its nearly vertical northwest face. The last glacier retreated about 10,000 years ago, revealing Half Dome's distinctive profile.

Blazes on the trail of an ancient glacier, erratics—boulders and rubble frozen

in the moving ice and deposited when it melted—abound near Olmsted Point.

Glaciers etched the Yosemite high country. Fine particles of rock moving under thousands of tons of ice scraped and polished the granite. Flakes weather from the shiny surface, leaving glossy patches (opposite) that gradually disappear. Over millennia rain and wind have softened the sharp edges of a chunk of granite near Olmsted Point (above).
FOLLOWING PAGES: *Lichens, first life to return to the ice-razed wilds of Yosemite when the glaciers retreated, mottle a granite boulder.*

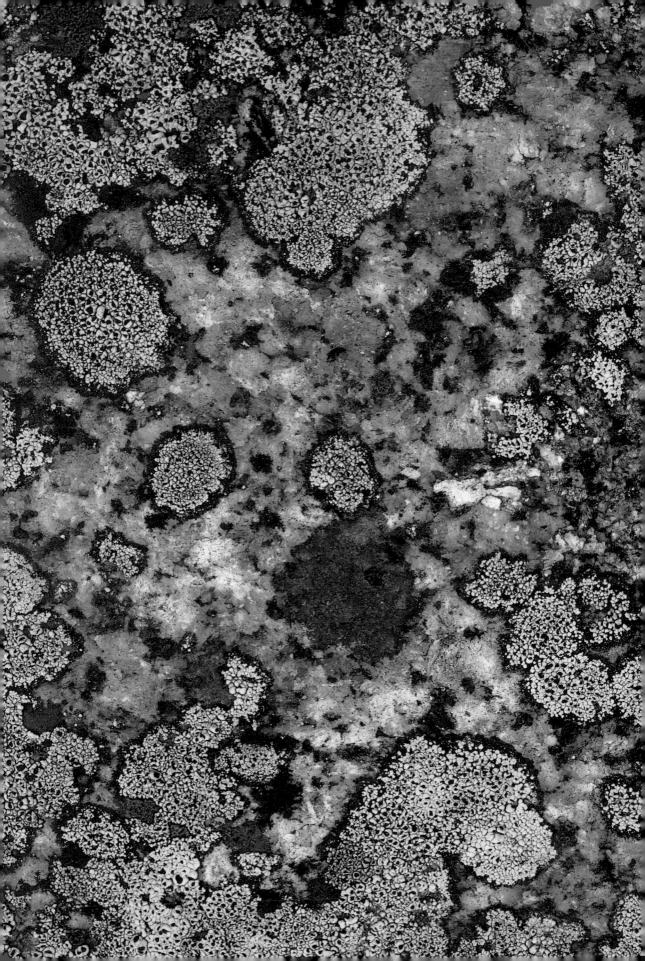

Panorama of the power of ice: Steep granite ramparts wall mile-wide Yosemite Valley;

from Half Dome it sweeps west past El Capitan seven miles to the Wawona Tunnel.

Man in the Park

*T*he Yokuts, early inhabitants of Yosemite, had a theory for the creation of the Sierra. There was a time, Yokuts storytellers said, when the world was all water. At about the spot where Tulare Lake now lies, a tall pole stuck above the surface. Atop the pole perched a hawk. Above the hawk hovered a raven. As soon as the hawk had made himself comfortable, the raven would swoop and knock him off. As soon as the raven had settled his own feathers, the hawk would dive and knock him off. And so it continued, for age on age.

Wearying finally of this exercise, the hawk and the raven created the birds that prey on fish—the pelican, eagle, duck. One small duck swam down to the bottom, came up with a billful of mud, and died on the surface—stricken by an early case of the bends, perhaps. From mud in the dead duck's mouth, hawk and raven formed the Sierra Nevada.

A nice, simple theory. No plate tectonics, no batholith, no glaciation; just a pole, a hawk, and a raven. *(Continued on page 46)*

Atop Overhanging Rock, the brink of Yosemite's Glacier Point, motorists in a Studebaker roadster enliven a 1916 publicity shot. White men first entered Yosemite in 1851 to rout the Indians; tourists soon followed.

Tabuce, a beloved interpreter of Indian culture at the Yosemite Museum, worked there from 1929-42. Pictographs on a granite wall (above) hint at prehistoric Indians whose origins in the valley remain a mystery. Carved on a lodgepole pine, soldierly graffiti depict crossed sabers of the 4th Cavalry, I Troop (right). The U.S. Army patrolled Yosemite from 1891, after it earned national park status, until 1914.

In 1875 a bumpy, two-day stage ride from the nearest train depot to Yosemite Valley

afforded bruised but happy passengers this vista of Yosemite from Inspiration Point.

In early October, the month of Yosemite National Park's anniversary, I followed Jim Snyder up into the country that hawk and raven made. Snyder is Yosemite's historian and archivist. His specialty is past inhabitants. We were looking for old signs of man in the park.

The trail led us past Virginia Lakes and up toward the park boundary. The scant lakeside meadows were dry, the tussocks turned pale gold, the willows yellow gold, the bilberry scarlet. The higher ridges were dusted with snow. The red metamorphic rock of Gabbro Peak and Epidote Peak looked hard-edged and Martian against the dark, otherworldly blue of the autumn sky.

*U*nderfoot the trail felt wonderful. It had been too long since I had been in my home mountains. Lately my career had taken me nearly everyplace else, it seemed. Now was a good time to be returning—just before the centennial, and in autumn, when the mosquitoes and the hikers are gone from the high country.

Snyder and I were woefully lacking in mountaineering chic. We were not going pretty into the mountains. My pack was a 23-year-old Kelty that had knocked about from the Galápagos Islands of Ecuador to the Brooks Range of Alaska. Jim Snyder's was an REI model 20 years old that looked brand-new. Snyder's job as archivist is a recent development. For 25 years, until 1987, he worked on Yosemite trail crews, which are supplied by mule. He has lived his life in the mountains but has done little backpacking, and his old pack looks almost virginal.

Contouring Blue Lake, I saw us suddenly from a remove. We were two characters lost in time and only now emerging.

James Snyder is a fair-skinned man about five feet eight. He has muttonchop whiskers that are mistaken sometimes as homage to Muir, one of his heroes. Other times they are assumed to be imitative of the whiskered cavalrymen who patrolled Yosemite late in the last century—the period that interests Snyder most as historian. The truth is more prosaic. Jim Snyder has spent much of his life sunburned, without hot running water, and shaving has been a pain. He is 45, and the red of the sideburns is now shot with gray. Snyder's legs are short, but his step is quick, and he has long experience in covering ground. He did not yet look the archivist, I could not help noticing. He still looked the trail-crew foreman: high-topped leather boots, blue jeans, a faded plaid shirt, and a silvery metal hard hat with the emblem of the National Park Service.

We left Frog Lakes and climbed toward Summit Pass. My feet were growing a little warm. I had forgotten the correct sock combination for my old boots, and we had 12 miles to go, but I wasn't worried. I never get blisters. It felt as if a little gravel had got inside and worked itself down toward the toes. I planned to empty the boots when I got the opportunity. Just below the pass we met three day-hikers coming down. They were to be the last people we would see for several days. The backcountry now was ours. From the pass we descended a little, then climbed to the bench that holds Summit Lake. The country of crumbly red metamorphic rock was ending. To the west lay the pale, unyielding granite of the true Sierra. At the western end of Summit Lake, we crossed into Yosemite National Park. Snyder was now in his proper domain.

We stopped by the lake, just inside the boundary, and ate some lunch. I unlaced my boots and upended them. No gravel fell out, and I peered in, surprised. I felt my socks, but no grit adhered. Checking the balls of my feet, I saw patches of red. I *had* been too long away from these mountains. I was finally to learn what blisters feel like, it seemed. I pulled on an extra pair of socks.

From Summit Lake we descended into Virginia Canyon. The canyon was thickly forested with lodgepole pines. On the flatter stretches of the canyon floor, the tawny autumn grasses grew high under the lodgepoles—a feature which, a century ago, drew sheepherders and their flocks. The sheepmen in turn drew cavalry, whose mission was to flush them out. Where the walls began to steepen, the grass gave way to dwarf manzanita. On these better drained slopes, an occasional western white pine now grew among the lodgepoles.

We turned right up a side canyon, left the trees, and crossed an open, alluvial slope of white-granite gravel. The gravel was softened by tussocks of sedge, dry and golden now in October. Crushed granite makes poor soil, and the sedges grew in fairy rings, their circumferences expanding as the sedges exhausted the nutrients at the center. There came stretches where dry meadow of sedge completely obscured the gravel, but we could still feel the crushed rock underneath. "Like walking on snow," Snyder said, and it was true. The crunch of gravel, under the softness of sedge, felt exactly like walking on snow.

"People come to the mountains looking for different things," Snyder went on. He waved in the direction of the creek. "Backpackers like camping down by the stream. They don't know—or don't care—that it's 10 or 20 degrees colder there, and wetter. The sheepherders liked it farther back. They wanted some trees, places where they had some view of their sheep. And they liked spots where the valley made a neck, a constriction. That made it easier for them to watch their animals. The Indians usually preferred open, sandy flats like this one, away from the bugs."

We passed through an avalanche scar—a tangle of fallen lodgepoles, a few fallen hemlocks among them—then came out in another slope of gravel and fairy rings. Halfway across, Snyder stopped in his tracks. At his feet lay a piece of obsidian. He stooped and picked it up—a "blank," flaked from a larger piece of rock but as yet unworked into arrow point or scraper. Paiutes from the east side of the Sierra probably had brought it here for trade with the Miwok of the west. The obsidian lay right where his theory of Indian preferences predicted, in the middle of a sandy openness. "I'm interested in the different places people chose," he said. "The different reasons. There are *layers* to this park." He tossed the obsidian back. It fell almost exactly where it had lain for centuries, black, angular, and anomalous against the white roundedness of the gravel.

*T*he oldest artifacts uncovered in Yosemite are the work of ancient people who arrived around 1400 B.C. For a couple of millennia these hunter-gatherers, whoever they were, had the valley's beauty to themselves. Slowly, over the centuries, the monoliths and monuments of the valley walls were humanized by their lore. The pale, ice-carved granite faces accreted an overlay of myths, legends, associations, explanations. Around A.D. 1250, the early inhabitants were replaced by new tribes, people who left behind a new material culture. The granite faces of the valley were scraped clean, as if by glacial ice, of myths and associations. The humanizing of the monolithic walls began again from scratch.

Throughout Yosemite's long prehistory, this razing and reworking must have occurred many times; mythology recapitulating geology.

The first tribe for which we know the name—the last to call the valley its own—was a band of Miwok who named it *Ahwahnee,* "the Place of the Big Mouth," for its shape, and called themselves *Ahwahneechee,* the people of that place.

The Ahwahneechee, like other Miwok, built conical structures of several sorts—dwellings, assembly houses, acorn granaries, sun shelters, sweathouses. The Miwok sweathouse, hemispherical, earth covered, and cramped, did most of its business with deer hunters. The deer hunter entered the sweathouse before dawn and stayed for as many as three hours. Outside, as he straightened

48

from his sweathouse crouch, the high granite of El Capitan began to catch the first sun. A thousand feet of granite wall beside Yosemite Falls glistened with rime—spray frozen there overnight. The incense of the cedars was muted in the cold morning air. The hunter ran, his skin steaming, through the forest of still-dark pines. He crossed the meadow and jumped into the icy current of the Merced.

Jim Snyder and I carried our sweathouses on our backs. Occasionally, as we labored under our packs down Virginia Canyon, I heard Snyder give a little grunt of protest, but he never slowed down. He wanted to be in camp by nightfall. Here and there along the skyline, the forested slopes of the canyon ended in smooth, steeply angled exposures of granite. The granite was as pale as the lodgepole pines were dark. It was below the granite, I noticed, that all the avalanche scars lay. The slickrock had provided no anchor for the snow. It was off the slickness that the snowslides had broken loose and rumbled.

The avalanche scarring was fresh. There was more of it than I remembered ever seeing. It all dated, Snyder said, from March 1986. In that year, an entire winter's worth of snow had fallen in six weeks, and the sibilant rush of avalanche had sounded everywhere. We passed through the first scar, a cleanly delineated zone of bent and prostrate lodgepole pines, all pointing downhill. We came to the biggest scar of all. Its avalanche had been so momentous that it had crossed the bottom of the canyon and had flowed up the far side. Here the tips of the bent and flattened lodgepole pines pointed uphill.

There was no snow now in Virginia Canyon, but I could imagine it: The wave front of the avalanche tumbling to catch up with salient tongues of itself; the hissing roar; the muffled, machine-gun crack of thousands of trunks; the avalanche cresting like surf up this far side of the canyon; the great cumulus of snow crystals rising, then thinning; the sun dogs sparkling prismatically.

"We're coming through these canyons just about 156 years to the day after Walker came through," Snyder said. "Lucky for us we don't have the snow year he did." Joseph Walker and his trappers were the first white men in the Yosemite country; the first whites to see, if not exactly to discover, Yosemite Valley. The exact route of the Walker Party is still debated, but Jim Snyder believes it crossed Virginia Canyon. Pointing downcanyon to the south wall, he showed me the route of the old Indian trail he believed Walker must have followed.

Joseph Rutherford Walker was born in 1798 in Tennessee and moved west with the frontier to Missouri. He was a dark-skinned and powerfully built six-footer, quieter and less boastful than most frontiersmen of that era. In the summer of 1833 Walker and about 50 men split from the trapping expedition of Capt. B.L.E. de Bonneville in the Rockies, and with four horses apiece and a year's supply of trade goods and ammunition they headed for the Pacific. By October they were climbing the east side of the Sierra Nevada, teams of men and horses alternating in breaking trail through deep snow. The horses had little food. The men ran low themselves and began butchering the horses. Once over the crest, Walker probably descended by way of the divide between the Tuolumne and Merced Rivers, in what is now Yosemite National Park.

"We travelled a few miles every day, still on the top of the mountain . . . ," Zenas Leonard, Walker's clerk on the expedition, would write. "We began to encounter in our path, many small streams which would shoot out from under these high snow-banks, and after running a short distance in deep chasms which they have through ages cut in the rocks, precipitate themselves from one lofty precipice to another, until they are exhausted in rain below.—Some of these precipices appeared to us to be more than a mile high. Some of the men thought that if we could succeed in descending one of these precipices to the bottom, we might thus work our way into the valley below—but on making several attempts we found it utterly impossible. . . ."

The Ahwahneechee, who detected the trappers passing to the north, believed that they had failed to see the valley. In fact, as Walker would later testify, his party knew very well that a great valley lay below them, but nearly barefoot and close to starvation, they were in no condition to explore it.

*A*s we descended a steep and rocky stretch of trail, Jim Snyder half-turned. "Miners came in here with burros," he called over his shoulder. "It had to be some kind of genius, without a map, to bring vegetables in on a route like this." Our boots were braking hard against the steep slope, but our imaginations had skipped ahead in history.

For nearly two decades after the Walker expedition, Yosemite and its hidden valley remained a secret. Then gold was discovered in California. The foothills filled with prospectors. The Indians were under the illusion that the country was theirs; the prospectors knew better. They took their usual potshots at Indians; the Indians took umbrage. There were the inevitable raids and counterraids, with the inevitable results. In 1850, a trading store on the Fresno River was raided by Indians, and the men running it were killed. The store belonged to the first Caucasian luminary of the Mariposa hills, a man named James D. Savage. Savage had begun as a prospector, but like other astute men of the period had soon seen that greater profit was to be made in commerce with miners and had opened two stores in the gold country. After the raid on Savage's store, the governor of the new state of California authorized the formation of a volunteer militia, "the Mariposa Battalion." Savage was appointed major.

Most California tribes accepted treaties, but several did not. Among the recalcitrants were the Ahwahneechee, also often referred to as the "Yosemetos," or "Yosemites." The Ahwahneechee, according to the treaty Indians, inhabited a secret valley in the Sierra, and would never come out willingly. In March of 1851, Major Savage and two companies of his Mariposa Battalion set out after them. Savage followed a route very close to the present Wawona Road to the valley. Messengers went ahead to demand the surrender of the Yosemites. The chief of those renegades, an old man named Tenaya, showed up at Savage's camp. He promised Major Savage that his people would surrender. Savage waited three days, grew impatient, and set out for the secret valley with Tenaya as guide. The most impressionable of Savage's men was a 27-year-old named Lafayette Bunnell.

On March 27, 1851, at the spot Bunnell called "Mount Beatitude" and later visitors would call Inspiration Point, Yosemite Valley suddenly opened before the Mariposa Battalion. I have surveyed the valley from that beatific and inspirational point, as have millions of other 20th-century visitors, but for Bunnell the view was brand-new, pure serendipity, an Old Testament sort of revelation. "The grandeur of the scene," he would write, "was but softened by the haze that hung over the valley,—light as gossamer—and by the clouds which partially dimmed the higher cliffs and mountains." It was Bunnell who suggested that the valley be named Yosemite, after the natives. Within two years they were forced to flee the piece of home geography that had given them their identity.

An astonishing thing about Yosemite is the speed with which it went from prehistory to present. In 1851, the valley was Ahwahnee, a secret valley known only to the Indians. By 1855, the Ahwahneechee were gone, and the first tourist party had arrived. Among those tourists was Thomas Ayres, who made the first sketches of Yosemite. Four years after Ayres, C. L. Weed arrived with photographic apparatus. Just eight years out of the Stone Age, Yosemite had entered what is essentially its modern era—the Age of the Sightseer and the Camera.

On June 30, 1864, 13 years after Ahwahnee became Yosemite—31 years after Walker first saw the valley from above—President Abraham Lincoln signed the Yosemite Grant, which entrusted Yosemite Valley and Mariposa Grove to the state of California "upon the express conditions that the premises shall be held for public use, resort and recreation, shall be inalienable for all time."

Yosemite became de facto—eight years before Yellowstone became officially—our first national park.

The old lore of the Miwok had faded. A new lore began attaching itself to the Sierra landscape: The story of Black Bart, who robbed stages with an unloaded shotgun, retiring between robberies to a gentlemanly life in San

Francisco. The tale of the Bactrian camels that traveled through the mountains to work in the Nevada mines. The stories of Galen Clark, guardian of Yosemite, and J. M. Hutchings, the hotelkeeper, and John Conway, the trail builder.

The sheer granite walls of Yosemite Valley and the High Sierra, erased of their Miwok legends, had become blank slates again. Geologists came, read the marks on the granite, and began elucidating a lore of their own.

Albrecht Penck, grand old man of European geomorphology, was so moved at seeing the fault escarpment on the Sierra's east side that he asked his guide to leave him for a few hours so he could be alone with it. For Penck and scientists like him, the old hawk-and-raven theory of the Yokuts would no longer do. They sought other explanations for the origin of the Sierra. California state geologist Josiah Dwight Whitney began his studies of Yosemite in 1863. Whitney became convinced that Yosemite Valley had been created by the sinking of a block of the earth's crust. The granite domes of the Yosemite country had formed, he thought, as giant bubbles of fluid granite. Whitney's assistant, Clarence King, found evidence of a glacier in the valley, an ice river a thousand feet deep, but Whitney dismissed this possibility, and King himself missed the importance of glaciers in the making of the valley.

William P. Blake of the University of Arizona was the first to move away from natural catastrophe as explanation for Yosemite. He proposed that the valley was carved by a torrential river flowing underneath a valley glacier. Blake was getting warmer — or colder, technically — as the correct answer lay at the low end of the thermometer.

John Muir entered the mountains with an open mind and a good, self-trained, naturally rebellious intellect. Everywhere Muir wandered in the Sierra, he saw signs of ice: glacial moraines, glacial polish, glacial gouges and chatter marks, and the ice-transported boulders called glacial erratics. He found remnant glaciers themselves, 65 of them, "sheltered beneath broad frosty shadows, in amphitheaters of their own making. . . ." Within a year of settling in the valley, Muir began advancing a theory that tied glaciation to its origin. "Nature chose for a tool not the earthquake or lightning to rend and split asunder, not the stormy torrent or eroding rain, but the tender snow-flowers noiselessly falling through unnumbered centuries. . . ."

Wandering the high country with Muir's books as my guide, reading the old glacial marks, I have sometimes *seen* those vanished rivers of ice.

In John Muir, Yosemite had found its principal explainer, poet, and advocate. Muir was born in 1838 in Dunbar, Scotland. When he was ten, his family moved to a Wisconsin farm. It is difficult to say at which end of himself Muir's genius lay, his head or his feet. The head trusted the feet, following them in long walks, first across Michigan to Canada, then from Indiana on a thousand-mile walk to Florida. He intended next to explore the Amazon, but he could find no ship bound for South America and sailed for California instead.

From Oakland, Muir walked across the wildflower fields of the San Joaquin Valley to Yosemite and there found his place. "No temple made with hands can compare with Yosemite," he wrote. "Every rock in its walls seems to glow with life. . . . Awful in stern, immovable majesty, how softly these rocks are adorned, and how fine and reassuring the company they keep: their feet among beautiful groves and meadows, their brows in the sky, a thousand flowers leaning confidingly against their feet, bathed in floods of water, floods of light. . . ."

*I*n upper Virginia Canyon, Jim Snyder and I stopped before a lodgepole, the tree Muir called the two-leaved pine. The lodgepole is the commonest and least aristocratic of High Sierra pines. One feature that distinguishes it is the two-needle bundle of its foliage. Another is the ease with which it takes an ax blaze. No one would have stopped by this particular lodgepole except for the yellow blaze seven feet up the trunk.

Snyder invited me to look closely. Inside the blaze, carved in thin lines with a knife, was a cross with triangular extremities engraved more than a century ago by a Basque. The Basques were, and are today, the great sheepherders of the West. "A cross like that has 'sheepherder' written all over it," Snyder said. The Basque cross, more than any other blaze, marks out the ranges of the Basque herders, according to Snyder. From the distribution of the crosses, he has deduced that the Basques and their flocks entered the Sierra from the east side and concentrated their grazing in Tuolumne Meadows and the Tuolumne River drainage.

"Here's Our Lady of the Mountains," said Snyder. Under the cross, a voluptuous woman had been crudely but respectfully carved. She is wearing what Snyder takes to be a bustle and high collar.

Inside Snyder's pack were two cameras, a compass, a measuring tape, a tree-coring auger, and a clipboard and a stack of forms for recording blazes. He did not bother to bring any of this out for Our Lady of the Mountains. He had recorded her—blaze No. 125—on a previous trip.

We next stopped, some distance down the trail, at a "T" blaze. The T, Snyder told me, was a cavalry blaze. It was in use from 1895 to 1914. The joke in those days was that the T meant "Trail" and enabled troopers to find their way home. The men who blazed the T came in pursuit of the men who blazed the cross. Grazing was illegal in Yosemite National Park. (Muir called sheep "hooved locusts," for they did enormous damage to Sierra meadows.) When the cavalry encountered sheep, they arrested the shepherds and turned their flocks loose, driving the animals out the east side of the range.

*W*e stopped again at the mouth of Spiller Canyon, at blaze No. 141, a skull and crossbones. Snyder takes it for a territorial mark. He guesses there was a warning in it: This canyon is mine; stay out. The skull was effective. It was spooky in several ways. For one, the blaze was scarring over, with bark impinging on its margins; the skull seemed imprisoned, trapped in the tree and staring out. For another, the blaze was carved in an unfamiliar style, an idiom different from skulls we draw today. The teeth were a row of X's. The round eye sockets had pupils carved there, thin and vertical, like those of a cat.

In the next days we found and recorded dozens of blazes. Many were the kind Snyder has termed "directional"—the T of the cavalry, for example. A few were "religious," Basque crosses mainly; a few were "pictorial," like Our Lady of the Mountains; a few were "territorial," like the skull. Most were "personal," dates and initials that said, by other names, "Kilroy was here." The blazed trees were archives. For Snyder, Yosemite's archivist, the high-elevation, open-air records of the lodgepoles are at least as interesting as the mustier kind kept indoors. The blazes were another way men had of humanizing Yosemite's wild country. They were a reminder that wilderness is never truly that.

In our fourth day in the Yosemite backcountry, Snyder and I finally met another human being. He was a young man recently discharged from the Navy. He had sought out the mountains as antidote for the confinement of shipboard life. Now, after a few days of solitude, he was almost giddy to see us and eager for talk. Travel in the Sierra wilderness is lighter today than it was in the boom years of the 1970s. Yosemite Valley grows more crowded, but traffic on the park's remoter trails is thinning out. That is fine with me.

On our fifth day, descending from a small, unmarked pass that divides

McCabe Lakes from Saddlebag Lake, we met two climbers on their way up. They were the last people we were to meet. The climbers wanted to try some ice routes; they had not decided which. They nodded in the general direction of North Peak, the 12,242-foot arête immediately west of us. There were some sheer snow chutes on North Peak, blue-white in the shadow, looking icy indeed. But Mount Conness and its glacier lay beyond—perhaps they were thinking of that.

The two were going in the Day-Glo colors of state-of-the-art climbing gear. Their backpacks were of space age materials, with crampons and carabiners and climbing helmets tied to the outside. We parted ways, the climbers resplendent, Snyder and I dowdy in our worn boots and ancient packs. Each pair of us was secretly pleased, I think, at how we looked in contrast with the other.

Climbers do their own sort of humanizing of the blank slate of Yosemite's walls. Where the casual visitor sees bare monolith, where the Indian saw the features of mythical heroes and legendary forebears, where the geologist sees exfoliations and old evidence of ice, the climber sees routes. The more difficult of Yosemite's walls, for the climber, are all ramified with dotted lines that none of the rest of us sees. On the west face of El Capitan, for example, there are the routes called "Realm of the Flying Monkeys," "Mirage," "Lurking Fear." On the southwest face there are "Squeeze Play," "Lost World," "Pacemaker." On the southeast face lie "Tribal Rite," "New Jersey Turnpike," "Eagle's Way."

The charters and namers of this strange vertical geography congregate in Yosemite Valley. The valley offers the most difficult rock-climbing in the lower forty-eight and is mecca for climbers all over the world. The namers and charters, the pilgrims, take jobs with the concessionaire—Yosemite Park and Curry Co.—and with the National Park Service to be near the granite. You can detect them at a distance—two young men, say, in the uniforms of Ahwahnee Hotel grounds keepers, pausing in their duties to discuss some pitch on a route they are planning, their hands climbing and traversing like those of fighter pilots describing dogfights.

The lives of rock-climbers depend on the subtlest depressions and prominences in the granite. No group, not even the geologists, has been on more intimate terms with Yosemite's raw materials.

Above Saddlebag Lake, Jim Snyder and I turned to watch the two climbers head up toward the pass we had left. Beyond them the blue-white snow chutes on North Peak looked almost vertical.

"Geez, they can have it," said Snyder.

"I couldn't agree with you more," I said.

I thought of the Indians, the trappers, the shepherds, the climbers, the backpackers, artists, archivists, writers. It is fascinating, as Snyder had observed, the different things that people come seeking. There are, in his words, *layers* here. Yosemite is parks within parks within parks.

Stately groves offer "luxurious scenic banqueting." The rhapsodic phrases

of innkeeper J. M. Hutchings launched Yosemite's tourist trade in 1855.

Prospector, innkeeper, philosopher, Galen Clark lived among Yosemite's largest stand of giant sequoias, which he surveyed and named the Mariposa Grove of Big Trees. It became part of the nation's first state park in 1864, when President Lincoln signed the Yosemite Grant. Guardianship of California's new public domain went to Clark. The grove's Wawona Tree (opposite) drew visitors from around the world. The Mariposa Grove Museum (below) stands on Clark's cabin site.

"Everybody needs beauty as well as bread," insisted naturalist John Muir; he achieved his greatest triumph—the establishment of Yosemite National Park—in 1890. At age 70 (left), he faced five years of battle to halt construction of a dam (top) in the Hetch Hetchy Valley of the Tuolumne River. Congress voted the dam (above) in 1913; Muir died a year later.

The Living Park

*I*t has become a family ritual. We park near the Tioga Pass entrance, at Yosemite's eastern boundary. My father chats with Ferdinand Castillo, the gatekeeper. Ferdinand, for most of 36 summers as a ranger, has been a sort of St. Peter at this entrance. He is Yosemite's most famous modern eccentric. He maintains a butterfly cemetery at Tioga Pass, giving a decent burial to monarchs and swallowtails he peels from the grills of entering vehicles. He stops long lines of cars so that frogs can cross. He is a ferocious guardian of the meadows around his gate—best not to stray from his paths.

Ferdinand waves good-bye. We set off on foot for Dana Plateau, my father leading, my mother following, me bringing up the rear. My parents go slowly, and this seems strange. When I first followed these two up into the mountains, it was the other way around—the struggle for breath was all mine. We cross meadows, pass through groves of lodgepoles. Timberline falls behind. We feel the altitude, puff a little. Just in time, the gradient levels off in the anomalous, windswept flatness of the Dana Plateau. *(Continued on page 68)*

Spring, lavish but brief in Yosemite, crowds a low meadow with lupines.
Flowers bloom later in the High Sierra; buds open in late summer
and early autumn. Most flora and fauna thrive in the lower elevations.

63

*Sierra still life: A fleeting leaf rests against a granite boulder in Bridalveil
Creek. Gentle much of the year, the stream surges with melted snow
and summer rains, bringing cascades to Bridalveil Fall. Maple-leaf gold
(above) lights the striated cinnamon bark of an incense cedar.*
FOLLOWING PAGES: *Low-lying mist and morning sunbeams brush distant
Half Dome and silhouette a lone elm in a valley meadow.*

Dana Plateau is one of those islands in the Sierra that were never glaciated, and this gives the place the feel of belonging somewhere else. The plateau ends abruptly in a precipice. Nowhere is the suddenness of the Sierra Nevada's eastern escarpment more dramatic. In shadowy places along the edge, summer snow lingers, deeply pitted with sun cups. Straight down, thousands of feet below, bone-dry, a-shimmer, lies the desert of the Mono Basin. I remember how strange this paradox seemed when these same two people introduced me to it: snow in summer. A taste of arctic chill in the California desert heat.

*O*ne virtue of mountains is the escape they offer from latitude. If a trail into the peaks makes a kind of time tunnel — an avenue back into the wilderness that preceded man, or forward into the wilderness that will follow him — it also makes a telescoping passageway, a warp in space, that admits him to other latitudes, far faunas, different climates.

Yosemite National Park begins in the Upper Sonoran Zone, where the walker would think himself to be, for all the world, in the heat and dryness, and among the plants and animals, of the Sonoran Desert. Climbing to about 4,000 feet, he passes into the Transition Zone, a country of ponderosa pines, incense cedars, white firs, moderate winters. At about 7,500 feet, he enters the Boreal Zone, where the trees are stunted, the pelage plush, the winters long and harsh, as in the high latitudes of the planet. The Boreal Zone is divided into subzones: the Canadian, where the walker finds himself somewhere in southern Manitoba or Saskatchewan; the Hudsonian, where he finds himself at the approximate latitude of Hudson Bay; and the Arctic-Alpine, where he finds himself beyond timberline somewhere north of the Arctic Circle. The Sierra's higher peaks and passes, in their climatic regimes and biology, are like islands of the Arctic broken off and drifted south.

The Upper Sonoran Zone covers the foothills on the west slope of the Sierra between 500 and 4,000 feet. Summers are hot. Winter snows are light. It's a country of bull pines, oaks, yerba santa, greasewood, and manzanita; of pocket mice, kangaroo rats, California jays, tarantulas, and rattlesnakes. For many travelers to Yosemite — myself, I have to admit, sometimes among them — the great pleasure of the Sonoran Zone is getting out of it.

The portals of Yosemite Valley are not just an unfolding of one of the finest scenes on earth, they are a gateway to the Transition Zone and to temperate latitudes. They mark an exit from the heat, dryness, and cicada hum of the zone below. There are those who believe, of course, that too many pass through those portals. The valley is visited by 3.5 million people annually. Each spring, as sure as the melting of snow and the reappearance of marmots, newspaper features ask: "Can Yosemite Survive?" There are strong arguments that Yosemite Valley, finest expression of the Transition Zone, is on its way to becoming an expression of something else.

I believe that Yosemite will survive. When I ask myself why, I recall a walk I took in spring, seven months before commencement of the centennial. With no particular goal in mind, I left Yosemite Lodge and walked downvalley. I passed the parking lot—not quite full—then the reception building, then the last cabin. In ten minutes civilization was behind me. Beyond the gas station and the last campground, I turned into the forest. My feet brought me to where a trace of asphalt showed through a thin duff of ponderosa needles and oak leaves. The valley was reclaiming old road. The reclamation would have been complete had not the feet of deer and bears and humans worn a path through the duff, keeping a narrow remnant open. This reversion was, I thought, an encouraging development—or undevelopment. I set off through the ponderosas.

The ponderosa pine is monarch of the lower elevations of the Transition Zone, king of Yosemite Valley. It is a robust and tall tree, large specimens reaching 200 feet or more in height. The bark in old ponderosas is furrowed into large, russet-red plates composed of layers of thin scales. The twigs are brownish and smell like orange rind. The yellow-green needles come three to a bundle and are 5 to 15 inches long. The ponderosa does not ask for much in the way of soil. It likes well-drained, gravelly earth under it but is indifferent as to type—limestone, basalt, sand, clay. Its extraordinarily deep roots allow it to prosper in dry country, and it does well on burned-over land. It prefers level or rolling terrain, growing tallest on the U-shaped floors of ice-carved valleys.

As a seedling, the ponderosa needs a little shade and generally comes up in the shadow of its parent. Full grown, it wants unbroken sunlight. No tree in the Sierra gives back more light. On still days each terminal tuft of needles is a glittery bundle of shards of sunlight. On breezy days the mountain wind choruses and coruscates through the crowns like fire. If, as Muir declared, the Sierra is "above all others the Range of Light," then the ponderosa is, above all others, the quintessential Sierra tree. "This species also gives forth the finest music to the wind," Muir went on. "If you would catch the tones of separate needles, climb a tree." Who but Muir would have listened attentively enough to hear the tones of separate needles?

My trail through the groves of singing pines followed close along the valley's northern rim past a jumble of granite boulders. The talus had stopped as if

69

against a wall. In rockslides like this one, along the margins of the valley, the mountain king snake has its dens. The king snake is especially fond of hunting the leaf litter under Yosemite's canyon oaks. It is the most beautiful of Sierra snakes, banded alternately in red, black, and yellow. Docile in human hands, it is hard on rattlesnakes—one of the few natural enemies of those vipers.

The boulders of the slide were not the white, clean-faceted boulders of a recent rockfall. They were dark and mossy, detritus from some old exfoliation of the cliffs above. And yet they seemed alive. They were like an army halted. Now and again it seemed to me that the rock army had jumped a bit closer when I was not paying attention.

The trail now led through a mixed forest of ponderosa and incense cedar. Ponderosa and incense cedar, growing amiably together, are the dominant trees on the floor of Yosemite Valley. They are edging out the black oaks, which in their turn have impinged on the meadows, which reclaimed ancient Lake Yosemite, which succeeded the Pleistocene ice. This latest stage in the valley's evolution, like the previous stages, won't be the last. The valley is never quite complete. The cedar foliage glowed a warm yellow-green. The big white blossoms of dogwood shone in the darkness of the understory. The foliage of the black oaks, bright and backlit, made illuminated borders to the clearings. The big-leaf maple, backlit even brighter, made illuminated borders to the streams.

The trail angled away from the cliffs, crossed the road, ran along the bank of the Merced, then entered a dark grove of ponderosas. In the grove I met a coyote trotting businesslike in the other direction. He scarcely glanced at me but swung a little wide to make room. I turned and followed. The coyote, looking back only once, seemed not the least uneasy to have me tailing it.

I took this for another encouraging sign about Yosemite. The fearlessness of park animals is one feature of high visitation that critics seldom talk about. Wild animals become so accustomed to unarmed, well-behaved humans in Yosemite that they behave as if no human were there. You might have entered some magical blind of the subtlest construction, all sign and scent of you erased. The animals are not tame, just oblivious. They go about their business. It's unnatural behavior, in one sense, but entirely natural in another. You look deeply into the iris of the wild eye, yet the eye hardly records you at all.

The *uzumati* of the Miwok—the grizzly bear that once dominated the Transition Zone—is gone. The last California grizzly was killed in 1925. The wolf and condor are gone as well. European man is quick to eliminate big predators in competition with himself. But all the rest remain. The black bear is here still, and the mountain lion, the fisher, the eagle, and the porcupine. The wolverine is rare now, but it always was. The bighorn sheep has been reintroduced. The coyote seems more plentiful than ever.

I trailed my coyote until it trotted out into the lush May meadow. Soon only its head and shoulders showed above the tall grass. I sat on a log at the meadow's edge and watched the coyote hunt. It pounced twice but caught nothing. It moved steadily upvalley, and I watched it diminish until only the ears showed above the green sedges. It was most likely after meadow mice.

The meadow mouse, or vole, is the common mouse in Yosemite Valley. It is a large mouse, short tailed, with long pelage, dark brown above and gray below. Its eyes are small and weak, its whiskers sensitive and discerning. It lives a split-level existence. Underground, it digs tunnels in the wet black humus of its meadows; a shallow labyrinth of mousewide passageways, complete with side pockets or turnarounds, short dead-end spurs, sump tunnels angling downward for drainage, and, at the heart of each system, a spherical nest of clipped grass. Aboveground, the mice cut a network of runways through the meadow, and along these they forage. The runways are exactly that. Pursued, the mice race the turns and straightaways almost faster than the eye can follow. Often, the stems and blades of bordering plants arch over to make a green arbor that screens the runway from hawks and coyotes.

*I*n their tunnels and runways meadow mice are reasonably safe, but not invulnerable. Now and then the paws of a coyote crash, gigantic, through the green vault of the runway arbor. Now and then an owl pitches itself off a branch in the darkness of the ponderosas. It flies low over the meadow, the grasses skimming away beneath in starlight amplified by the night-scopes that owls have for eyes. The owl, detecting motion on a runway, drops on muffled wings and lifts away a mouse.

Sometimes in summer the terrifying, brown, musky rush of weasel comes coursing down the runways. Sometimes in winter the skylight of a ventilation shaft frames a portrait of the same predator—the low, rounded ears, the acute, triangular face, the implacable intent, the fur changed with the season—as white now as snow. The skylight darkens, the sun ceases to glitter in the snow crystals at the entrance, and the glitter now is all in the eyes of the weasel.

The weasel's design, from the point of view of meadow mice, is diabolical. Built long, pointy, low to the ground, and just an inch or so in diameter, it is camouflaged brown in summer, white in winter. It is as supple and sinuous as a snake, but without the snake's modest food requirements. The weasel—bad luck for mice—has the high metabolism and big appetite of warm-blooded creatures. It is all speed, reflexes, and hunger.

Like weasels, moles are present throughout Yosemite, from the Transition Zone to the Hudsonian. In the meadows of Yosemite Valley they are numerous. The mole has the look of a creature being sucked inside itself. The neck is gone already—the long snout seems to emerge directly from the shoulders. The eyes and ears have disappeared in fur. The mouth has migrated south. The forelegs are so retracted that they lie alongside the head. Turn-of-the-century zoologist Joseph Grinnell, an authority on the mammals of California, described this body plan as an "entering wedge." With a short, powerful breaststroke, the mole travels rapidly just under the surface of the earth. From the deep burrow system in which it nests, the mole sallies forth on shallow foraging expeditions, swimming the soil an inch or so below the surface.

*T*he shrew is the mole idea miniaturized and set loose in another medium. The shrew has the long snout, the sensory whiskers, the weak eyes, the unpleasant taste, and the raging metabolism of the mole. It lacks only the digging forefeet. The Yosemite shrew is common in the valley and elsewhere in the Transition Zone. It is the second largest of Sierra shrews. This is not saying much—the Yosemite shrew's body is not quite three inches long, with two inches more of tail. Like other shrews, it inhabits damp environments: meadows and thickets beside streams. It is a micro-carnivore. Captive shrews have been known to eat their own body weight every three hours. In the wild, shrews eat insects, centipedes, lizards, mice, snails, carrion. Life is an endless sequence of Chinese dinners—the dishes varied, exotic, insufficient, the shrew always hungry five minutes later.

The southern pocket gopher is the common gopher on the Yosemite Valley floor. The pocket gopher lives a productive and satisfying life. It works long, hard days in mountain air, its nose in the fragrant Sierra earth. Few creatures are on such intimate terms with the terrain—the good Sierra grit on its incisors, the taste of the mountains on its tongue. Into every burrow, of course, some bad must someday slither. The five-foot length of a gopher snake enters silently, endlessly; thick bodied, the color of dry grass. The tunnel fills up with the subtle but terrifying scent of reptile. The gopher snake is a constrictor; all it wants is a little hug. If the gopher fails to find an exit quickly, it departs its own passageway for a more constricted one. The snake unhinges its jaws, and the gopher goes spelunking headfirst down the tunnel of the snake.

Sometimes the circle of sky at the burrow entrance is divided by the white streak that parts the face of badger from crown of head to nose. The teeth and foreclaws go to work, the tunnel fills with the chuffs and grunts and musk of badger, and rapidly, alarmingly, the circle of sky grows larger. The badger torso is thick and muscular, the legs short and powerful, the feet huge and armed with long, sturdy claws.

The trail I followed left the meadows of Yosemite's small mammals and led again along the river. I came to where a white, angular block of granite lay five feet under the clear, greenish water of the Merced. It was one of those rare, ambitious boulders that have jumped far beyond their colleagues in the talus. It was a measure of how narrow Yosemite Valley truly is, even after its gouging out by ice: This rock, spalled from the rimming cliff, had bounced all the way into the middle of the stream. There was no telling the age of the boulder. The cold current had kept it as clean and white as if newborn, freshly broken from the cliff. I remembered how, at the age of two, I had wandered off to explore the valley. The hotel maid had asked my parents if they had checked down by the river. My mother must have imagined something like this: something cold and pallid under the fast, greenish eddies of this snow-fed mountain stream.

The trail traveled some distance through the forest, then came out in full sunlight. It skirted a meadow and passed through a herd of mule deer—four does and two young bucks. They were grazing in an isthmus of forest between this meadow and the next. After a glance at me the deer, like that coyote earlier, seemed to forget I was there. They were feeding very selectively now, in the plenty of spring, among unfurling ferns and clumps of bunchgrass in the ponderosa shade. First one, then another of the elegant heads came up. The sleek black noses took turns testing the various breezes. While its fellows grazed, the sentinel-of-the-moment would swivel its great ears to fix on some infinitesimal twig snap from the forest. Once all the heads came up simultaneously, and all six pairs of ears swiveled. Something of great interest to mule deer had occurred across the meadow, on the far side of the Merced. I peered that way, listened hard, detected nothing. Yosemite's mule deer winter in the Upper Sonoran and in summer move up into the Transition and Canadian Zones. They go quietly, on small hooves that seem designed for silence.

The range of *Felis concolor*, the mountain lion—or puma, or cougar—is exactly that of the mule deer, its principal prey. The lion's migrational rhythms are those of the deer, as are its diurnal rhythms—active in morning and evening, drowsy at midday. The deer and the lion are complementary propositions. Both are spotted in infancy; both grow into a tawniness. The two have been competing in silence, and in detecting little failures of silence, for hundreds of thousands of years. They have an old, ongoing contest to see who can go fastest from a standing start to top speed.

El Capitan showed through the trees. The trail swung closer to that greatest of Sierra monoliths, and its impossible verticality rose higher and higher above the crowns of the pines. I searched the vastness of the southeast wall for climbers and finally found them, or found their bivouac—a speck of color halfway up the wall. The scale was too vast to make out human figures.

The hammocks and sleeping bags of the bivouac were tied into the vertical rock. Wisps of mist were forming—materializing from thin air—at the level of the bivouac, then growing into small, fast-ascending clouds that swept up and over El Capitan's brow. The rock is so tall that its parts have different weather, different seasons. Here at the bottom it was spring—I was wearing a T-shirt—but up where the climbers toiled, 1,700 feet above, it appeared to be winter still. Now and again the forming mist obscured the bivouac completely. I imagined the climbers, cold hands on cold granite. I felt the sentiment that is nearly universal among watchers at El Capitan's base. I was glad I wasn't up there.

I crossed the El Capitan bridge and headed back upvalley. Nearing Yosemite Lodge, in an airy stretch of ponderosa forest, very open in the understory, I came across a pair of coyotes. They were trotting the springy ponderosa duff, one trailing 40 yards behind the other. I spoke to the second coyote as it crossed a log. It paused to look at me, then stretched and yawned. The yawn may have been one of those nervous canine yawns that mask small moments of anxiety, or maybe it was just a plain yawn. Then the cabins of the lodge showed again through the trees. I had completed a circuit of the better portion of the valley floor. I had met six mule deer, three coyotes, several squirrels, two chipmunks, a number of flickers, more Steller's jays than I wanted to count, and just two human beings—a pleasant young couple of Middle Eastern extraction.

Those who see ruin in Yosemite have it exactly wrong, in my opinion. It seemed to me miraculous that I could pass, in a narrow valley visited by millions, an afternoon as uncrowded as this one.

Beyond the confines of the valley, the western slope of Yosemite rises through stands of white fir and sugar pine to the realm of the giant sequoia. That tree, monarch of the upper elevations of the Transition Zone—indeed monarch of the entire planet—is *Sequoiadendron giganteum*, the Big Tree. *Sequoiadendron* is the largest organism that has ever lived. It belongs with the dinosaurs back in the Jurassic and the Cretaceous, the age of giganticism. "The king of all the conifers in the world," wrote Muir, "the noblest of the noble race. . . . The Big Tree is nature's forest masterpiece, and so far as I know, the greatest of living things."

The old genus *Sequoia,* from which the Big Tree, after much debate, was divided 50 years ago, once covered most of the Northern Hemisphere. In the Cretaceous, ancestral sequoias grew in the Arctic—giant forests well beyond the planet's present timberline of stunted spruces. Only two species survive. One is the coast redwood, tallest of trees, which persists in a narrow fog belt along the northern California coast. The other is the giant sequoia, most massive of trees, which retreated to lower elevations of the Sierra to escape the Pleistocene ice and now survives in moist spots of the range.

A sequoia seed, sprouting, sends down a slender taproot, then unfurls its first leaves and throws off the cap of its seed hull. For eight years or so, the root grows downward faster than the seedling grows up. Then downward growth ceases, and thereafter root spread is all lateral. Aboveground, through the first century of its infancy, the tree is conical, its bark gray, its limbs drooping, its foliage blue-green. In its second century, or its third, it begins to take the "pole form": the trunk bare of branches for a distance above the ground, the branches near the crown ceasing to droop. The foliage goes greener, and the branches near the crown form elbows. After a millennium or two, the tree joins the fraternity of the giants: bark reddish brown and deeply furrowed, bole 20 feet in diameter, the branches trees in their own right. The largest Big Trees reach about 40 feet in diameter and 300 feet in height. On the biggest sequoia stump he ever found, John Muir spent a day with a pocket lens and counted more than 4,000 rings. "I never saw a Big Tree that had died a natural death," he wrote.

The secret of this everlasting life, perhaps, is in the Big Tree's outer bark, a corky, fibrous, deeply furrowed, reddish brown cortex overlying the thin integument of the inner bark. In old trees, the outer bark is two feet thick, and it might as well be asbestos. Only when a fuel of lesser trees and understory shrubs accumulates close to the trunk can fires burn with enough intensity to work through to the wood. The giant sequoia likes fire. It needs occasional small fires to burn away accumulated fuel around it. Its seeds need the occasional cool fire to burn away the forest duff, as they germinate only on bare, mineralized soil. (What the sequoia does not need is conflagration.)

Black bears sometimes den in fire-hollowed giant sequoias. They make mattresses of shredded sequoia bark, or moss, or sugar-pine boughs, and sleep through the cold months. Higher up, the Douglas squirrel, or chickaree, nests in loftier hollows of sequoias, or renovates old woodpecker holes. It is the high-construction worker of Yosemite, comfortable in sequoia crowns 300 feet above the earth. Vertigo is not among its liabilities. Chickarees are as muscular as the gray squirrels of Yosemite Valley, but more lithe, agile, and a third the size. Their territory is primarily the Canadian and Hudsonian zones, whereas the gray squirrel's is the Upper Sonoran and Transition. The belt of the sequoias marks the border between. The chickaree is the noisiest inhabitant of the sequoia groves, with a query that goes *quer-o?* The squirrel emphasizes each question with body English, flicking its tail into an interrogation mark. If the chickaree is not satisfied with your answer, or is startled by it, it emits a piercing, scolding, whickering squeal and skitters loudly up its sequoia trunk, claws sending down showers of the bark's translucent and papery outer scales.

The chickaree eats the flower buds of conifers and the tips of the young twigs, but its specialty is the cones. The naturalist Lowell Sumner once counted 41 squirrel-clipped cones dropping from a sequoia in five minutes. At the peak of the fusillade, 13 cones hit the ground in 10 seconds. The giant tree and the tiny squirrel have worked out a symbiosis. Of the millions of cones hidden away under logs by chickarees, many are forgotten. In return for its meals, the chickaree plants trees. The chickaree's is a fine life. There are the pleasures of insulting and berating anything that passes by, bombing assorted creatures who imagine they are nobler beasts than squirrels, dwelling rent free in cool, green, Doric mansions. There is a downside to this upper-story life, of course. Sometimes, when a chickaree has cut its score of cones and is racing headfirst down a sequoia to retrieve them, there comes a louder, faster skitter of claws overtaking, then the fast-closing musk of marten.

The pine marten is a large, dark weasel common in the Hudsonian. It is an occasional raider of the upper Transition Zone and the Big Trees. The marten is just under two feet long, including the bushy tail, and weighs about three pounds. On ground, it travels with a bounding élan. In trees, on sharp claws curved to catch in bark, it has the speed to outstrip the chickaree. The chase spirals round and round the trunk, out across the boughs, from tree to tree.

Sometimes the marten, intent on the squirrel intent on pursuing its cones, hears the scrape and scritch of bigger claws behind it, smells the fast-closing fraternal musk of fisher. The fisher is the next biggest in the weasel line. The fisher is something close to that perfect predatory organism of science-fiction horror movies. It comes with sharp, curved claws for tree travel and can sprint headfirst down conifer trunks. It seems unfair, but those bark-gripping claws protrude from all-terrain feet. The paws are thickly furred between toe and foot pads for travel on snow, and they are rapid, too, over summer earth. On the ground, the fisher bounds along like some nightmare squirrel, nine feet at a jump. The fisher is king of the sequoias—as the sequoia is king of trees.

In the Mariposa Grove of Yosemite there was a great sequoia, the Wawona Tree, so enormous that the road passed through it, a rectangular tunnel cut through the base. As a child I never liked passage through the tree. I understood then, even better than I do today, that the tunnel through the tree was wrong, an insult. Cars grew larger—Detroit's brief, golden age of beaminess—and the road was routed around the tree. My father, David Brower, was then executive director of the Sierra Club. The new, wider road was cut too close, in his opinion. He worried about the tree's roots, and, indeed, in the unusually heavy snows of the winter of 1968-69, the Wawona Tree fell.

*L*ater that year, my father left the Sierra Club and founded a new organization, Friends of the Earth. A colleague collected cones from the Wawona Tree and shook out the seeds. To charter members, my father sent a letter of thanks; affixed to each was one of the seeds. "A GIFT FROM THE TREE (and from Friends of the Earth)," the letter began. "One day, about two and a half millenniums ago, when things were just right for it, a small seed began the process of putting together the exact amounts of air, water, soil, and solar energy to form what would be the Wawona Tree. Most of the seed was a wing, to carry it far in the wind. Within the seed itself was a wealth of vital, unique, secret information, packed with great efficiency in a very little space. It would inform the tree and all its parts, specifying . . . a long list of things a tree ought to know, each essential, none superfluous."

Seeds of ponderosa and fir and incense cedar are similarly voluminous, of course. Each contains the same long list of things a tree ought to know. The fertilized eggs of bear and mouse and weasel are also packed with vital information, each item essential, none superfluous. Yosemite is more than its granite walls and waterfalls. It is an encapsulation of North American flora and fauna, with affinities that reach from the Sonoran Desert to the High Arctic. It contains, in each of its plants and animals, an unbroken sequence of successes stretching back some three billion years to the origins of life on the planet. It is a representative piece of the system—wilderness—in which we ourselves trace our own unbroken chain of success. That is why, perhaps, it is always so joyous to walk home into Yosemite's mountains again.

Swollen with snowmelt, the Merced River near Leidig Meadow mirrors a Yosemite

spring—bold conifer green and the tint of new leaves on water-loving willows.

Lichens and mosses transform boulders and fallen trees into a velvety Eden. The generous cupped leaves of Indian rhubarb lend a tropical look to a mountain stream. Tourists seeking the imposing spectacle of towering rocks and waterfalls within the park often discover another Yosemite—smaller in scale, equally dramatic, and constantly changing.

Robust and wary coyote wears a thick winter coat. The animals roam valley meadows

and roads; their sharp barks and melodious howls pierce tranquil parkland nights.

Valley visitor preserves a moment spent with a mule deer. Black bears—
Yosemite's largest carnivores—wander throughout the park, often
frequenting campgrounds in search of food. The creatures grow accustomed
to humans and lose their fear, which threatens their independence.
FOLLOWING PAGES: *Largest living things on earth and among the most*
enduring, giant sequoias share space in Mariposa Grove.

Gossamer mist from Nevada Fall veils a primeval pine forest.
The Merced River, following the ancient path of Ice Age glaciers,
feeds the waterfall with spring and early summer snowmelt
from the High Sierra. Sweeping summer and autumn fires clear
deadwood and promote new growth; a vigorous shoot sprouts
on the charred bark of an incense cedar.
FOLLOWING PAGES: Corn lilies form a profuse garden of green.

Great gray owl perches on a fir snag. Often seen at twilight, the birds hunt

small mammals in meadows and clearings. Dead trees support staghorn lichens.

As foothill meadows of grasses tassel and dry in early summer, blue-violet
brodiaea lilies reach their peak of bloom. Indians once harvested the small
lily bulbs and baked them in earthen ovens. A male red-winged blackbird,
resplendent in bright epaulets, clings to an upright stalk of dried grass.
Dense stands of willows, tules, and grasses in freshwater marshes
along the lower Tuolumne and Merced Rivers attract the birds.

*Mountain plants have an adaptive elegance and economy
that increase with elevation. At more than 10,000 feet, Sierra
primroses nestle in granite crevices (opposite). Stonecrop's waxy
leaves store moisture (top). Fiery snow plants (above, left)
feed on decayed matter. Monkeyflowers (above, right)
flourish from the foothills to above the timberline.*

Ice crystals sheath a spray of meadow grass in the Tuolumne high country.

On average, Yosemite's winters bring 29 inches of snow to the valley below.

The High Country

*A*t about 7,500 feet in Yosemite, a walker leaves the Big Trees behind. The air grows thinner, the timber sparser, the winds freer, the vistas wider, the snowdrifts deeper in shady places. The walker, a little short now of breath, departs the temperate world and enters the near far north of the Boreal Zone. He is a bit winded, maybe, but his boots are magic boots, spanning leagues of latitude with each upward stride. That walker, in some of the happiest times of his life, has been me. In the high country, for me, the time-space warp of mountains gains an extra dimension. My first memories are of the High Sierra. Each visit there is personal time travel, a return to the very beginnings of myself.

The first memory, I think, is of arrowheads in a high meadow. None of the points is perfect. The dry margin of the meadow glints everywhere with half-buried shards of obsidian—black volcanic glass. Most, on being dug out, prove to be flakes spalled off by Paiute or Miwok fletchers long ago, but here and there among them lies a point that was almost finished, *(Continued on page 106)*

Alpenglow at moonrise illuminates the jagged crests of the Cathedral Range. Most of the park lies above 7,500 feet—a rugged domain of alpine meadows, glacial lakes, mountain vistas, and lofty solitudes.

Beyond the sunstruck summit of Half Dome, a summer snowstorm
obscures the craggy wilderness of Yosemite's High Sierra. To gain this view
visitors drive up Glacier Point Road and hike to Sentinel Dome, a monolith
pocked with eroded basins. Boulders rim the shore of one of the Young
Lakes (above), where anglers can cast for brook trout.
FOLLOWING PAGES: *Sawtooth Ridge stands sentinel over Yosemite's remote*
northeast corner, a section of the park few tourists visit.

nearly triangular, before an ill-aimed stroke spoiled it. The fletcher tossed it away angrily in the Stone Age; I pick it up wonderingly in the first decade of the Atomic. The edge is still sharp. For him it was trash; for me it is treasure.

From that meadow of arrowheads, the trail switchbacks down, fresh still in my memory, through the deep dust of summer. I lead the way, knees bent, feet shuffling, boiling up great clouds of dust. A sharp word from behind, and I come to understand—a little surprised, somehow, though this is my third warning—that my parents are not so delighted by my dust cloud as I am. My father shows me how to lift my feet straight up, then set them down again without sliding. This is how one is supposed to walk when dust is deep. It is my first lesson in good trail manners. I take some pleasure in perfecting the step, but not half the pleasure I took in the bad manners preceding it.

*T*hat night, or some other night of that trip, I encounter the universe for the first time. Tired from the day's walk, I am supine in my sleeping bag, looking up. In camp at 11,000 feet in Yosemite, interstellar space seems blacker. The stars burn brighter, in all their thousands. There are five, ten times as many stars as at home. The arc of the Milky Way crosses from one horizon to the other, nebulous but unbroken, like a bridge you might cross. The stars shine a little too bright. They are closer, more intimate, and they speak to me, but there is nothing intimate or friendly in what they have to say. They whisper of inconceivable voids and distances, of impossible heat and cold, of infinity. At sundown in high mountains, the temperature plummets as the stars multiply. I find the drawstrings and tighten the mummy bag about my face. The cold comes like a wind from the stars. The interstellar void smells faintly but sharply of pine needles, and its chill is on my cheeks. I know I should sleep, but I want to keep looking. I practice closing my eyes once or twice. When I open them again, the sky is pale blue with dawn.

The forests down in the Transition Zone are beautiful places. There is the music and refulgence of the ponderosas, the fragrance of the cedars, the giant, abiding presence of the sequoias. There is the doe in the meadow, the squirrel on its log, the woodpecker drumming, the jay on its branch. Yet in the end, for me, there is also a kind of pleasant, low-grade claustrophobia in the trees.

I am hardly aware of it until I am released; until the dappled half-light of the forest gives way to the alpine sun.

As I followed Jim Snyder, Yosemite's archivist, up Spiller Canyon in our hunt for evidence of man in the park, the forest thinned around us, and I felt that old release. We were traveling cross-country, for there are no trails in Spiller Canyon. Our feet were free to find their own route. For a time we followed a glacier-smoothed expanse of slickrock bisected by Spiller Creek.

Whether flowing white in cascades, or in clear current over stones, or through the deep, mossy meanders they cut in alpine meadows, Sierra streams are beautiful. Nowhere are they more so, I think, than where patiently, over millennia, they have carved their chutes and sluices and channels and spillways in glacier-polished granite. Alongside the main groove of the creek, here and there in the slickrock, were shallow potholes. Stones, caught and condemned to roll for ages in the millraces of spring, had inscribed tight circles, grinding out basins for themselves, then finally had escaped.

Moving through the forest again, we came to a blazed tree. Snyder stopped to study and measure it. My attention, I found, was divided between the human history and the natural. As Snyder said, there are many layers to Yosemite. While he worked, my eye fell on a small granite boulder. The boulder, mostly quartz, was luminously white against the darkness of the conifers beyond. It seemed an Arthurian sort of stone; there should have been a sword embedded in it. But there was no Excalibur. Arthurian stones were scattered all over the hillside. This was simply the one my eye had fallen upon.

I noticed, near Snyder's foot, the cone of a western white pine. The cone was light and airy, like something you might find under a wood-carver's bench. It might be the carver's first try at a Christmas ornament, or a toy he had fashioned to amuse his child—the scales feathered from a scrap of blond wood with quick strokes of a gouge. I pulled a white-pine twig close and studied the fascicle—the bundle—of the needles. How considerate of the Designer of Pines, I thought. How helpful, these diagnostic little bundles: western white pine, five needles in a bundle; ponderosa, three needles; lodgepole, two needles.

The first of the zones in the high country, the Canadian, covers most of Yosemite. It is a country of red fir, Jeffrey pine, western white pine, and lodgepole pine. The tree emblematic of the zone, probably, is the lodgepole. The lodgepole is the Proteus and the Phoenix of western trees. Its protean nature— its changeability of form—bedeviled several generations of plant taxonomists. The scientific name *Pinus contorta* and the common name "lodgepole" summarize the problem nicely. *P. contorta*, through most of its range, grows anything but contorted. It rises as slender and straight as any pine on earth. The same tree, in its high-elevation mode at timberline, grows bent and twisted, low to the ground, with gnarled and thickened trunk—anything but a lodgepole.

The Phoenix of trees is designed to burn. In the slender pole form, it grows in stands so dense that dead snags have trouble falling to the ground. A typical lodgepole forest is an even-age thicket of living trees rising from a pavement of snags. Then the bolt of lightning. Flames race up the slanting snags, up deadwood ladders of lower branches, and onward into the crowns, where they ignite years of unopened cones full of resin. The lodgepole forest disappears in a quick and cathartic fire storm. The resin sealing the cones melts. The roasted scales pop open; the winged seeds scatter on the wind. A new generation of lodgepoles springs up from the ashes of the old.

Lodgepole pines attract porcupines, which feed on the soft cambium inside a tree's bark. The thin-barked lodgepoles make easy meals for them. If the thinness of lodgepole bark simplifies life for porcupines, it simplified things, too, for the people who wanted to leave their marks in Yosemite. A stroke or two of an ax cut away bark and cambium from a lodgepole. The bark of other pines is discouragingly thick. "You don't get much of this kind of history below the lodgepole belt," Jim Snyder told me, at the next blaze.

A mile farther up the canyon, while the archivist recorded another blaze, I looked down, my attention again divided, into a pool below. Spiller Creek narrowed to flow musically over an eight-inch waterfall into the pool. The song of the little falls was high-pitched yet resonant—like water in a well. The falls aerated the pool in a tumbly froth of small bubbles. Downstream, two six-inch trout held position, one behind the other, their heads into the pool's current. The water was crystalline. On the rust-red granite boulders of the bottom, the trout cast shadows that seemed more substantial than themselves. It was the dark, trout-shaped, sun-haloed shadows that I had detected first. The slow finning of the trout seemed too lazy to hold them against the current, but hold them it did.

Farther still up the canyon, my eye happened on a yarrow flower. I realized that this was the last yarrow flower of the season. In Spiller Canyon I had seen no others. At high elevation, yarrow grows much smaller and braver than in the foothills. I smelled the flower—dry now and nearly scentless. Crushing one of the plant's serrate leaves, I sniffed at that. The leaf was ten times as pungent and yarrowy as the flower. I admired several red, incandescent, backlit clumps of bilberry. Bilberry likes to grow as trim around the edges and in the cracks of boulders. In autumn this trim—the lanceolate leaves of bilberry—turns redder than blood.

I gazed up at the granite ridge above us to the west. The white rock, all fractured by bluish gray shadows, curved against the deep blue of the Sierra sky. The ridge was like a broken moon rising over Spiller Canyon. Out of the corner of my eye, I caught movement along the creek—a bird flying low over the water and upstream. I knew from the flight plan, even before I turned, what it had to be. A water ouzel, as drab in color as it was bright in spirit, landed on a streamside boulder. It did its double dip, looking back at me, then flew on.

"He is a singularly joyous and lovable little fellow," wrote Muir, "about the size of a robin, clad in a plain waterproof suit of bluish gray, with a tinge of chocolate on the head and shoulders. . . . Among all the mountain birds, none has cheered me so much in my lonely wanderings,—none so unfailingly. For both in winter and summer he sings, sweetly, cheerily, independent alike of sunshine and of love, requiring no other inspiration than the stream on which he dwells."

Snyder was standing, putting his clipboard into his pack. "Ouzel," I said, pointing upstream to where the bird had disappeared.

"Yes?" said Snyder, smiling the little smile all Sierra folk reserve for ouzels.

At about 9,000 feet in Yosemite, the walker departs the Canadian Zone and enters the Hudsonian. The red firs and lodgepoles fall behind, and he passes into a high-elevation forest of mountain hemlocks and whitebark pines. The high-country tree I love best is the one that grows highest, *Pinus albicaulis,* the whitebark. This ultimate Sierra tree, the final pine of timberline, is sometimes called whitestem or alpine whitebark. The name "albicaulis" sits best with me. If the Hudsonian has an emblematic tree, it is that one. A pretty little tree in life, the albicaulis is exquisite in death. The bark of the tree lightens with age, and the deadwood is carved into delicate ridges by the elements. The pale, twisted branches strike dramatic poses against the granite of the far ridge, against the cloudless Sierra sky.

For Snyder, I learned, the thing about albicaulis is its smell. We were up in the belt of whitebark pine, investigating the ridge that rims Spiller Canyon to the west, when he pointed to a whitebark snag. "That's the smell of the high country," he said, "clean and spicy."

The Hudsonian is the zone of the arctic three-toed woodpecker, the pine grosbeak, the Clark nutcracker, the white-crowned sparrow, the Belding ground squirrel, the mountain lemming mouse, the marmot, the coney, the pine marten, the least weasel, the wolverine. In this fauna, as in that of the Canadian Zone, Bergmann's rule—one of those generalizations somewhat less absolute than scientific law—is in force. Bergmann's rule states that warm-blooded animals of a given group tend to be larger in colder climates to the north. Or to the south, in the Southern Hemisphere. (As an animal grows larger, its volume increases faster than its surface area. Since it is through surface area that body heat is lost, the more voluminous the animal, the warmer it stays.) Bergmann has a corollary application in the cold climate of the high country.

Of the pocket gophers in Yosemite, the largest, as Bergmann's rule predicts, lives highest. The alpine pocket gopher inhabits the Canadian and Hudsonian Zones and the lower margin of the Arctic-Alpine. More than any of its cousins, it is a snow gopher. In winter it extends its subterranean tunnel system up into the drifts. The snow tunnels are roomier than the earth tunnels. They permit the gopher to reach plants buried in the snow, and they serve as receptacles for dirt excavated in extending the subterranean system. In springtime, as the snow melts, the earth-filled tunnels are gently lowered to the ground. They lie there, meandering earth cores, until summer thunderstorms erase them. Generally they have a different color and composition from the topsoil on which they rest. As a boy I saw those inconformities on the forest floor—the castings, it seemed, of some giant and mysterious species of worm—and could never figure out what made them. In Yosemite's northern canyons, whenever Jim Snyder and I strayed from the trail searching for blazes, we stumbled across the enterprise of gophers. With every 30th step in Yosemite's dry meadows, the heel of your boot sinks into a tunnel.

The largest of Yosemite's shrews, true to Bergmann, dwells in the Boreal Zone. It is the navigator or water shrew, and it lives in and around fast-flowing streams in the Canadian and Hudsonian. At six inches long, including tail, and just two-fifths of an ounce, it is hardly a creature to cause the earth to shake at its passage, yet beside the other shrews of the Sierra, it is mammoth. The water shrew is a kind of minuscule otter. In danger, and in pursuit of food, it dives into the fast, frigid streams that are its livelihood.

The water shrew's oversize hind feet are sufficiently broad, and the shrew's two-fifths of an ounce is sufficiently light, that the shrew can walk on water. It is less given to this biblical feat, however, than to acrobatics under the surface, where it is as fluid as an otter, turning, darting, gliding. Like the sea otter, the water shrew has pelage designed to trap air for insulation. Tiny bubbles clinging to its black fur give the shrew a quicksilvery shine underwater. Scampering along the stream bottom, trailing bubbles, the shrew is an ectoplasmic apparition, quickly gone.

It has always seemed to me that Bergmann's rule, or a variation on that theme, is at work in human beings. It is not so much that body size increases in people dwelling farther north—though this sometimes does seem to be the case. It is more that *personality* itself expands. Somehow the long winters and big spaces seem to feed individuality, idiosyncrasy, and generosity. Alaskans, for example, have a way of seeming much larger than life. The hermit-trapper, slightly eccentric, is an archetypal boreal character. This tendency toward expansion of virtues and flaws seems to apply, too, in the high country.

For three nights in the canyon, Jim Snyder and I shared our dinners, fed logs into the fire, and spiked our coffee with brandy while we talked about characters in the mountains: There was Bill Sabo, the sawyer who had taught him trail work. As Bill got older and his teeth failed, he had carved himself new ones from manzanita. There was Murphy, Snyder's old trail foreman. After a reversal of roles, Murphy had become his crewman, and then his cook. Snyder demonstrated an old Murphy trick, upending our finished brandy bottle and "sweating" it by the fire, distilling out the last drop.

*M*y childhood summers high in Yosemite, like Snyder's, were full of Bergmann's rule characters. There was Norman Clyde, a throwback to the age of the mountain men. Clyde had more first ascents in the Sierra than anyone else. Well into his 80s, he carried 90-pound backpacks into the mountains. Inside were cast-iron pans, an ax, a wedge, a crosscut saw, a pistol, a little anvil for repair of hobnailed boots. Younger men—striplings from our lightweight age of freeze-dried stroganoff and aluminum pack frames—passed him as if he were standing still. He moved with a glacial slowness, but always got where he was going.

There was Bruce Morgan, owner of Mount Whitney Pack Trains. Morgan was packer for many of the Sierra Club "High Trips" on which I first saw the Sierra. He was a big, weathered man who preferred mules to horses, believing they had a superior intelligence to go with their superior strength. Morgan traveled the mountains with a brace of beautiful white riding mules, on whose backs he rode alternately, and whose names I have finally forgotten.

There was Tommy Jefferson, head packer under Morgan and later his son-in-law. Jefferson was a full-blooded Mono Indian, a genius with livestock and good with a guitar. I remember nights, campfires, and Tommy Jefferson singing, his dark Indian face under the brim of his Stetson. Tommy wore a denim jacket, the uniform among packers. His cuffs were buttoned, even as he played. (Packers never rolled up their sleeves; it must have been against some packer code.) His square brown hand traveled surely on the frets, and firelight reflected from the honey-colored lacquer of the guitar. The side of my face toward the fire was hot. The side toward the night was cool. This, I thought, was how it felt to be the planet Mercury—one hemisphere burning, the other cold. A log popped, and red sparks swirled up into the stars.

One day a bronco mule—the blinkered kind I had been taught to avoid— went crazy, spinning in a tight circle, bucking off its load. Pots and pans flew and clattered, livestock snorted, people scattered. I glanced at Tommy Jefferson's face and saw the look of pure joy. Tommy ran at the bucking mule and leaped on its back. He spun a revolution or two with the mule, his legs flung out horizontal by centrifugal force, then he bit the mule's ear. *"Remember me?"* he seemed to be asking. *"Yes!"* the mule seemed to answer. It was instantly calm and reasonable, its great sensitive ear clamped between Tommy's teeth.

*A*t about 11,000 feet in Yosemite, a walker leaves the last tree behind and strikes out across the imitation tundra of the Arctic-Alpine Zone. In the Sierra Nevada, this final stratum of life is broken up into islands atop the higher peaks. It is less a zone, as we normally think of one, than it is an archipelago. Mount Lyell is the Baffin Island in this scheme of things. Mount Dana is the Ellesmere. The other island-peaks of Yosemite— Conness, Hoffmann, Forsyth, Clark, Triple Divide, Matterhorn—are as wind-swept and cold-pruned as any barren-grounds in the High Arctic.

The country above timberline is a land of dwarfed shrubs such as heather and of alpine flowers—mountain sorrel, rock primrose, and alpine saxifrage. It's the land of the alpine chipmunk, the coney, the marmot, the ice worm.

But mostly it is a land of rock. As the Sierra rises through its life zones, it effects a steady distillation of itself, until finally it presents an essence: the clean, bare bone of granite—arête, massif, ridge, col, couloir, pinnacle.

It is a country of talus. The Sierra Nevada is young, as mountains go, but the range has undergone some aging, and talus marks the attrition. There is colossal talus—slopes of angular granite boulders the size of warehouses. There is giant talus—boulders the size of houses. There is "big-jump talus," as my father called it—rockslides traversable in big jumps from rock to rock. There is small-jump talus. There are several sizes of little talus—inferior grades less pleasurable to cross, for these rockslides are still sliding, forever moving underfoot. There is the miniature talus called scree, granite atomized in collisions between the larger sorts of talus. Scree is treacherous, always threatening to skate your feet out from under you.

I have been a runner of taluses. I am a talus-runner still, though not so fast or reckless as before. The hazard of talus-running is that not all the boulders have reached their angles of repose. Every seventh or eighth rock shifts as you land on it. The trick to talus-running is continuous calculation. Which of the next rocks looks solid? Where on the chosen rock is the center of gravity? (If a rock proves tippy, you want to have landed on the fulcrum.) As often as not, you make your decision in midair. If the chosen rock does move, which alternate rock will you jump to? And if that rock moves, what is your third choice?

A runner of taluses is running against the odds. If he keeps at it long enough, the day comes when three rocks move in succession, or four. Things then grow interesting. As the time available for each decision diminishes, options grow fewer. Only a shot of adrenaline—and that hormone's way of crystallizing judgment and slowing time—saves you a broken neck. Once, in steep talus below a pass, I saw a deer leg protruding from the boulders. It was a stark reminder that talus moves, that accidents happen.

I have always been drawn to talus. For a child, a slope of giant talus makes a separate, private world just fifty or a hundred yards from camp. He can disappear into the talus—vanish as quickly as a coney or a marmot does—and right under his parents' eyes. He finds himself alone amidst the pale, tumbled blocks and broken pillars of some titanic ruined city. The boulders are rounded on their old surfaces, fractured into clean planes on their new. There is endless variety in the shapes. In coming to rest against one another, the boulders make chimneys, tunnels, kivas, crypts, caves. Some are too narrow to fit into, some too spooky. A few are too paved with the dried dung of rodents. Some are perfect hideouts, complete with sentinel windows for peering down, unseen, at the speck of your mother nervously scanning the slope above.

In the talus I arrived at a fine, visceral understanding of geology. I came face-to-face, at any rate, with geology's paradox—the density yet ephemerality of its subject matter. I passed under poised monoliths the size of freight cars. Squeezing between gargantuan boulders, I entered gaps so narrow I had to breathe shallowly and turn my head sideways to pass. I crawled on my stomach under low granite ceilings weighing hundreds of tons. A rockslide is all arrested motion. What if, right now, this one should move again?

Exploring talus I have come upon the piles of droppings that mark the sunning rocks of marmots and the sentinel rocks of coneys. The animals themselves always disappear at my approach. (If I am drawn more to talus than to peaks, then it is the same for most High Sierra animals. The marmot and coney are only the most obvious. Cougars, pine martens, wood rats, and weasels are creatures of the talus too. I was unaware of this as a boy—I never saw any of the more cryptic creatures—but nearly every boreal mammal seems to find refuge in the ruined cities of the slides.)

Occasionally I have succeeded in climbing undetected above marmots. Every high-elevation marmot has a favorite flat-topped rock from which to watch goings-on while it spreads itself flat to catch the rays. The little death of hibernation lies ahead. In the short, sweet Arctic-Alpine summer, marmots try to soak up all the sun and vistas they can. Marmots are the largest representatives of the squirrel family in Yosemite. By the end of a summer's grazing and laying-on of fat, an adult weighs seven pounds or so. Spread out yellow-brown on its rock, it looks even larger than it is. When it sees you the marmot coalesces, gathering its feet under it, and gives its piercing warning whistle. It is ready to run, but reluctant. It would just as soon stay in the sun.

I have never succeeded in climbing undetected above a coney. The coney, or pika, or rock rabbit, is a small relative of the rabbit that inhabits rockslides in the high country. As a defense against the cold, the coney's ears have been reduced almost to the size of a guinea pig's. Coneys always know where you are in their rockslides. They reappear magically here and there, traveling among the rocks by secret passageways, to complain about you sharply.

The coney is surely the most beloved of creatures above timberline, and its piping call is the anthem of the High Sierra—mountain music. The coney's cry, like the marmot's whistle, is a carrying sound. The coney throws its body into each bleat, jerking forward and rising off the rock. Its ears appear, twitching up and forward with each effort. Sound travels poorly over rugged and windy topography. Alpine animals—coney, marmot, chamois—tend to have outsized, piercing voices. Alpine humans, for their part, invented the yodel. It was with one of those, finally, that my father would call me down from the talus. His standard come-home yodel, or a fancy one, if he felt in the mood to hit the notes, would go echoing around the cirque, find its way into the deepest recesses of the rockslide labyrinths. Reluctantly I would come talus-hopping down.

There are fishermen—several friends of mine among them—who believe that the essence of Yosemite lies down in its Hudsonian and Canadian Zones. If it could be boiled down to some irreducible kernel, they would argue, the Yosemite experience would reside in the bright colors of a hand-tied fly settling lightly in the shadow of the far bank. This is a legitimate viewpoint, I suppose. For me, though, the essence lies up in the region of rock and snow and sky.

Climbers would argue for the peaks. The culmination of the Sierra, they would insist, is in the summits; the ultimate and quintessential Yosemite experience lies in achieving those. I have done some climbing, and I know what they mean. There is courage in it, and nobility sometimes, yet in the end no one has ever come up with a sensible reason for climbing a peak. "Because it's there" has had to do. Sometimes it even passes for profundity.

I would argue for the passes. From the time of our first migrations, the pass has had real meaning for us, man and beast. There is an old emotion waiting at the pass. Ask Hannibal, ask the Inca and the Tibetan and the Paiute. The pass divides watersheds, both hydrological and historical. It opens up a whole new country, new possibilities, and it closes an old country off behind.

The passes of the High Sierra tease you. Just another hundred yards to the top, it seems; just another hundred more. The highway through the high country north of the valley cuts through Tioga Pass. It can tease if your car is old and your radiator leaky, but it does not beckon and then withhold itself quite so maddeningly as those other Yosemite passes — the ones you climb on foot.

*T*he trail switchbacks up through bare talus. It crosses patches of pitted summer snow. Sometimes, nearing the top, there is no trail at all, just a procession of cairns. If you are out of shape, the climbing is misery. If you are fit, you have the pleasure of dropping into a lower gear and powering over. Finally, the trail ceases rising. A whole new country opens up ahead. You have arrived. Often a signpost, buttressed by talus, names the pass and notes its elevation. The post is a good place to rest your pack.

If there is snow, you make yourself a snow cone. You scrape the old-snow surface clean of any grit, any pink snow. The whiteness beneath is as dazzling and white as the day it fell. You crunch up a cupful of that and sprinkle your powdered lemonade on top.

You linger. You rest a while. You enjoy your accomplishment. These are perspicacious moments at the pass. It is only here, on the cusp, that you can see into the new country before you and the old country behind. Soon enough you will shoulder your pack again. Twenty paces down the trail, there will come a moment of regret as, turning, you see the old country vanish. There is always a small taste of sadness in leaving a pass.

I always try to find a comfortable rock near the signpost. I clasp my hands behind my head and look up. The deep-blue sky is empty above me, or flawed perhaps by a puff of afternoon cloud. The cloud sails eastward, dissolving at its edges. The Sierra, in rising through its life zones, has sublimed itself finally to that. Vapor. Sometimes, as I watch it, the vapor melts into nothingness. That is the mountaineer's nirvana, and the only one I seek.

Basking in an autumn sunset, the Tuolumne River curves through Tuolumne

Meadows, at 8,600 feet a popular base for High Sierra treks and day hikes.

*High Sierra hikers relax at May Lake Camp, one of five backcountry tent
camps that provide food and accommodations for those who want
to travel light. Curling spray from Waterwheel Falls (right) begets
a rainbow in the Grand Canyon of the Tuolumne River.*
FOLLOWING PAGES: *Glacier-polished granite sweeps above Tenaya Lake;
Yosemite Indians called it Pywiack— "Lake of the Shining Rocks."*

In a world of white, a skier glides past lodgepoles along Horizon Ridge Trail;

increasing numbers of visitors traverse Yosemite's high country in winter.

*Heavy snows bring a deep hush to a sunset landscape of red firs south
of the valley. In the High Sierra, snowfall averages more than 100 inches
a year. Drifts linger into August at Upper Young Lake (above). Even in
summer, temperatures sometimes dip below freezing at higher elevations.*
FOLLOWING PAGES: *Designed to withstand cold and wind, pinecones with
a tough woody shell encase the seeds of lodgepoles, the predominant tree
in Yosemite's subalpine zone. A waxy covering insulates lodgepole needles.*

Winter casts a spell on a forest of red firs near Ostrander Lake, south of the valley.

A nearby hut offers overnight facilities to some 1,500 cross-country skiers each year.

Barren scarp of Echo Peaks (above) guards the northern end of the Cathedral Range. Such raw and rocky splendors reward those who set out beyond the valley on routes such as the popular John Muir Trail. A landmark along the way, shimmering Upper Cathedral Lake mirrors the glacier-cut contours of 10,940-foot Cathedral Peak (right).
<small>FOLLOWING PAGES:</small> *Fiery twilight defines the narrow cleft of Tioga Pass, at an elevation of 9,945 feet the highest automobile pass in the Sierra.*

Valley of the
Range of Light

Walking Yosemite Valley in spring, I came to the edge of a recent prescribed burn and felt a shock of recognition. The blackened stumps and snags were thickly carpeted all around with blades of new spring grass. Some might have perceived the scene as ugly, but I did not. Charred stumps and renaissance grasses are a subject I had been taught by an artist to see.

If artists have a function in the tribe, it is that one: to teach the rest of us to see. The artist who had opened my eyes to the stumps was Ansel Adams.

As a boy, I had watched Adams, the writer Nancy Newhall, and my father assemble a book called *This Is the American Earth*. The book had begun as a photographic exhibit that opened in the tiny stone castle of LeConte Memorial Lodge, on the valley floor, not a mile from where I now stood. LeConte Lodge was a sentimental spot for Ansel Adams. In 1920, at the age of 18, he had been its custodian, and his photographic career had begun in expeditions out from its granite fastness. *This Is the American Earth* was *(Continued on page 140)*

"The Yo-Hamite Falls," a lithograph published in 1855 from a drawing by Thomas Ayres, gave the world its first glimpse of the mighty scenery of Yosemite; the grand setting has since inspired legions of visual artists.

Artists have found a muse in Yosemite for more than a century. George Fiske (left), who needed a wheelbarrow to carry his cumbersome equipment, opened a photography studio in the park in 1884. A modern counterpart, William Neill (top), focuses on the curves of a Jeffrey pine atop Sentinel Dome. Chris Jorgensen (above, right) painted the giant sequoias in 1901. Recently an artist (above, left) captured Lower Yosemite Fall on canvas.

Flamboyant gathering of clouds and light enhances the heroic scale of German-born

landscape artist Albert Bierstadt's 1868 oil painting "Sunset in the Yosemite Valley."

the first of its genre—a large-format book of nature photographs. Coffee tables round the world would groan, one day, under the load of such books, but in 1959 the idea was new, and it was theirs—Adams's, Newhall's, and my father's. It was an enormous gamble. I remember the excitement of the three participants. There was an aesthetic intensity I had not encountered before, and have not encountered since.

Among the photographs in the book was an Adams image called "Burnt Stump and New Grass, Sierra Nevada." I remembered the print on the table at Ansel's studio. It was always illuminating to study a photograph over the master's shoulder—to listen to his exegesis, to watch him crop, with his hands or sheets of paper, until something quickened in the composition and it came to life. The right margin would come in another centimeter, then a millimeter more, and the composition suddenly had inevitability. There was no other way to crop it. I remember Adams's fondness for the inky blackness of the print's charred wood, and for the contrast of the sunlight in the grasses below it.

The only difference between the burnt stump of the photograph and those around me was that the photograph had been framed by a master. As I studied the stumps, some ghost of Adams began to frame those too.

No artist has had a destiny so entwined with Yosemite's as Ansel Adams. In summer of 1916, on his first trip to the valley, his parents gave him his first camera, a Kodak No.1 Brownie in a leather case. Among his early efforts was a photographic attempt on Half Dome. He climbed a crumbly old stump to get a better view and was about to press the shutter when the stump gave way. On the way to the ground, headfirst, he inadvertently took the picture. The horizon was perfectly level in the photograph, but the scene was upside down.

In his later years, Adams would muse over the good fortune that favored his work. "Sometimes I think I do get to places just when God's ready to have somebody click the shutter!" he said. This divine intervention seems to have been in force from boyhood, guiding his shutter finger even in free-fall from the stump.

Half Dome, and the problem of photographing that monolith, was to change Adams's understanding of the medium of photography. Early one morning, in spring of 1927, he hiked with Virginia Best, his wife-to-be, and several friends up to the Diving Board, a granite slab on Half Dome's west shoulder. On his back was 40 pounds of camera gear: a $6\frac{1}{2}$ by $8\frac{1}{2}$-inch Korona view camera, several lenses, 2 filters, a heavy wooden tripod, and 12 glass plates. His goal was to make a photograph of Half Dome, but he stopped to set up compositions along the way; for Half Dome he had only two plates left.

At 2:30 in the afternoon, he set up his tripod and composed his image of the monolith. To slightly darken the sky in the conventional way, he placed a K_2 yellow filter over the lens and made his exposure. He now had one plate left. As he replaced the exposed plate with the fresh one, he began thinking about how the print would look. He knew what qualities he wanted: a brooding cliff under a dark sky, the snowy skyline of Tenaya Peak crisp and white in the background. "I realized that only a deep red filter would give me anything approaching the effect I felt emotionally," he would later write. He attached his red filter, increased the exposure time sixteen-fold, as the filter required, and exposed his last plate. The result, "Monolith, The Face of Half Dome," became one of his signature photographs. "I felt I had accomplished something, but did not realize its significance until I developed the plate that evening. I had achieved my first true visualization! I had been able to realize a desired image: not the way the subject appeared in reality but how it *felt* to me. . . ."

*I*f the task of the artist is to teach us to see, then Yosemite has been more instructive of our vision than any landscape in the New World.

The first Yosemite artist, Thomas Ayres, arrived in 1855, four years after its discovery. His lithograph "The Yo-Hamite Falls" was the first published picture of the valley. The first watercolorist, James Madison Alden, arrived in 1859, as did the first photographer, Charles Weed. Carleton Watkins, the first photographer of genius, came in 1861. It was Watkins's work that truly brought Yosemite to the attention of the world. In 1863 Albert Bierstadt, already famous for his paintings of the American West, spent a month in Yosemite; he would return several times in the 1870s. Bierstadt's fondness for rosy, low-angle light, his dramatic—even melodramatic—use of day's first and last illumination, brought Yosemite landscapes—or landscapes based loosely on Yosemite—to the eastern art world. Thomas Hill came and painted his more impressionistic Yosemite scenes. San Francisco's wealthy had to own Hills; then recession hit the state, and the artist spent his last years painting Yosemite scenes for tourists. I grew up with a Hill on the wall above the family piano. It was a dark, not very energetic scene of Bridalveil Fall—a sample, I imagine, of his latter period.

And then there were the writers: Clarence King studied Yosemite geology and wrote his perilous, hyperbolic mountaineering tales. Muir studied the geology and wrote his passionate and sometimes purple prose.

Yosemite became a battleground of conflicting aesthetics.

It was inevitable perhaps, in a valley to which so many artists trooped, that the line would be drawn there. An old school of aesthetic enlightenment—or endarkenment, perhaps—met a newer school. Champions of the old school were Bierstadt, California state geologist Josiah Whitney, and Clarence King. Champion of the new was John Muir.

Howard Weamer, one of the finest Yosemite photographers of the present day, is a student of that conflict. After a brief career as a scholar, he took up the camera. An artist now himself, he knows the struggle inside out.

Weamer is a tall man with a long Muir-like beard. For 15 years he has been custodian of Ostrander Lake Ski Hut in Yosemite. He spends his winters skiing, photographing, and—every fifth day or so—rescuing some skier who has failed to show up for the night. The photographer enjoys the snowstorms he searches when cross-country skiers are missing. The storms make a pleasant but circumscribed world—the beam from his headlamp illuminating nothing but a flurrying wall of flakes five feet in front of his face. He never worries about getting lost himself. He knows every tree and gully in the vicinity of the trail.

"I was interested in what was happening in the 19th century with Muir and Josiah Whitney and Clarence King," he said. "King was particularly heavily influenced by the 19th-century English writer John Ruskin, both in writing style and perception. As Muir said, for Ruskin nature was 'made up of alternate strips and bars of evil and good.' It was all sublimity and blackness. What Ruskin was after was a fusion of science and aesthetics. It was an emotive kind of science, close, in a sense, to Muir, *except that it had the negative*. It had the blackness. And Muir couldn't abide that. Muir knew right off that the proposition of the sublime's being 'the confrontal of God face to face, as in great danger, in solemn, sudden death'—as one of these Ruskinians said—was not for him.

"I went out to Yosemite Research Library, which had an amazing collection of 19th-century travel literature. Yosemite then was a must-see. You simply could not claim to be well traveled without having seen Yosemite. I must have read 40 or 50 tourist narratives from the 19th century, and there it was, over and over again—the sublime, which was anything that was very deep, or high.

Steep, black. Vulcanism. Great natural catastrophes. Storms at sea. Lightning.

"The height of emotion—aesthetic or any other kind—was when you were in the most danger. That was when feeling was strongest. You were after the strongest feeling, but it had to be negative. It had to be an impingement on your personal safety. In Yosemite, these people who stood on Inspiration Point, emoting about this black abysm, all terror and gloom, were simply following that convention.

"Bierstadt has this great painting, 'Night at Valley View.' It is the classic black sublime. The moon in the upper left. The gnarled oak. Little fire. Indians around the fire. Beetling crags. A little moonlight striking the water, but 99 percent of the canvas is black."

I wanted, at this point, to pause a moment and sort out the players in the aesthetic and intellectual struggle Weamer was describing.

"So, on the one hand," I said, "we have Bierstadt, King, and. . . ."

"Ansel Adams," Weamer suggested, when I struggled for another name.

"And Ansel Adams," I repeated. I was not entirely convinced, and my voice betrayed it. "Well. . . ."

Speaking of "Monolith, The Face of Half Dome," Weamer said, "I mean, there's some pretty strong, powerful, dramatic black-and-white."

"Right," I said, but without a lot of conviction.

Weamer might be on target about "Monolith, The Face of Half Dome," but what about "Burnt Stump and New Grass, Sierra Nevada"? The burnt stump itself was a fine instance of the black sublime—natural catastrophe, lightning, solemn death, inky blackness—but what about those new grasses, full of sunlight, in the foreground?

"I mean, not entirely—not at all," Weamer conceded. "But he's got his black sublime. And so do I. I've got a picture of Half Dome with the light shining on the face of it. But what Muir knew so clearly is that if your first response is fear, fear separates you. Love does not grow out of fear. Love attaches and fear separates. And he didn't want people to be separate from nature."

In the summer of 1975, when Weamer sat down to write his dissertation on geology and aesthetics, the language wouldn't move. Progress was slow and tortured. He calculated that he would need to spend two more summers away from the Sierra to get the thing done. He chucked it all, took up his camera, lit out for the mountains, and hasn't been back to the typewriter since.

"My grandmother photographed," Weamer told me, of the origins of his second career. "She went all over the world. Photographed with an old Exacta. She brought slides back from Egypt, the Holy Land, Russia. I grew up on slide shows. I was fascinated. On my first backpacks in the '60s I carried a camera.

"I'm a 19th-century person. A lot of the modern stuff doesn't appeal to me at all. I use a large-format camera. A 4-by-5. I take five or six pictures a day. If I get five or six a year that I want to print, that's (Continued on page 150)

"El Capitan, Winter, Sunrise, Yosemite National Park, California, 1968"

Ansel Adams

A Portfolio

"I *knew* my destiny when I first experienced Yosemite," wrote Ansel Adams, remembering a boyhood trip into the Sierra Nevada in 1916. America's premier landscape photographer, Adams found his creative center in Yosemite. Aiming his view camera (above) at natural subjects, he created timeless images, both lyrical and brooding. His meticulous style, technical brilliance, and romantic eye allowed him to realize his goal of "affirming the enormous beauty of the world." After his death in 1984, a mountain in Yosemite was officially named for him.

"Monolith, The Face of Half Dome, Yosemite National Park, California, 1927"

"Fern Spring, Dusk, Yosemite Valley, California, circa 1961"

"Dogwood, Yosemite National Park, California, 1938"

"Thunderstorm, Yosemite Valley, California, 1945"

more than enough. The eye is always going. I'm always excited by what I see.

"People are constantly asking me at Ostrander Hut, 'Don't you get bored up here? I mean, this is your 15th year. How could you possibly not get stale?' But it's absolutely just always new there. Your perception changes. Every year, I see something 50 feet from the hut that I've never seen before. You could take that as a negative thing. *Pay attention! You've missed that for 15 years!* I don't see it that way at all. You're pleased to find something fresh and something different. It comes in with so much joy attached to its tail that you just feel honored, graced, with this new thing. I really don't think I've spent 15 minutes of my 15 years bored.

"I actually learned to use a view camera in wintertime. It was madness. I mean, cold metal, fingertips freezing off. In winter, shutters have to be clean or they jam up. With a bellows camera, the snow gets in the corrugations. In snowstorms, you need shades over lenses so snow doesn't get on them. I put old ski-pole baskets I find along the trail on my tripod legs so they don't sink into soft snow.

"The color in the sky in evenings! It's gorgeous color—reds and yellows and golds. And the trees absolutely catch fire. Nights in December and January are just unearthly. The colors are stunning, unbelievable—it's like you used a filter on everything. I'm out virtually every night at sunset. Unless there's some skier having trouble coming in."

*I*f Howard Weamer belongs to Muir's army, Bruce Klein, whose charcoals I saw in the Yosemite Valley Visitor Center, seems to belong to Ruskin's. In 1989 Klein was an artist in the Yosemite Museum's Artist-in-Residence Program. I liked his charcoals and thought I saw in them hints of the black sublime.

"The Artist-in-Residence Program got me back into Yosemite," Klein told me, when I tracked him down. "When I first came out to California from Indiana, I headed down to Yosemite and did a lot of camping. For me camping was this survivalist kind of test in the wilderness. You go with minimum food and minimum weight, and you live on the edge as much as you can. You push to your physical and psychological limits."

Klein, pushing himself to his limits, sounded very Ruskinian indeed.

"I use charcoals in a unique way, in the sense that I really get physical with the paper," he said. "There's a lot of erasing on it, and a lot of pushing charcoal around. By the time I'm done, I look like a chimney sweep. That's what engages me. Charcoal is a medium that's very hands-on; you use your fingers. There are finger marks, and erasures—all kinds of activity going on. In paint and in charcoal it's a very complex experience, trying to work in the valley—to capture the grandeur, the truth about the physical beauty of the valley, its monumentality.

"You climb up to the base of El Capitan. There's a little moraine; you can scramble up to it. Cold! You can look straight up, and you see these climbers, roped and dangling. You can hear these hammers way up there, and then, every once in a while, you hear some crazed guy screaming his lungs out. Some climber. You don't know how high he is. You're looking up, and there's water splatting you on the head, on the hair."

This settled the matter. The vast, cold verticality of El Capitan and that crazed guy screaming his lungs out were as darkly sublime as anything King ever wrote or Bierstadt ever painted. I knew to which army Klein belonged.

"There's a certain kind of physicality to that." Klein went on. "For me there's an attempt to get some of that physicality into paint and use the viscosity of paint to trap it. The way you can play thickness and thinness of paint and color against each other.

"I've climbed trees. I would climb the tree, then tie myself up there for safety, and stay there past sunset. You know, it's a little crazy to be up there after dark, when you can't see what you're doing. How are you going to paint up in a tree? But you go to see what the light looks like, to be there then, to have that range of experience. All that enters in. It's not just your eyes that the experience comes through. It's your sense of smell, and your taste, touch. The weight of things against your body. All that is used in my painting."

Muir, the anti-Ruskinian, did this sort of thing, of course. Muir liked climbing trees in gales. I was suddenly less certain as to which army Bruce Klein served.

"It's necessary to get off your duff and explore," Klein said. "To see things from a variety of angles. I like being out there. It doesn't matter if I'm painting. I like climbing around, and the wind in my hair, and I like the smells. I like to go out there and backpack. Being out there in the snow. The winter—I love that. I've been down there in the winter trying to paint trees, and it's driving me crazy. Trying to paint them. Out there by the side of my truck, out in the snow, my toes are cold, my fingers are freezing. I'm trying to do charcoal. When you work charcoal that cold, things break. Your fingers crack. Paint! I've had brushes freeze up in the acrylics, because I'm not working fast enough."

I had heard all this before. The craziness of working in Yosemite winter— the freezing fingers, the love of being outdoors whether doing art or not—

were all things that Howard Weamer, soldier of Muir, had confided in nearly identical language. Categories are probably a mistake. Extremes come around to meet, finally, and soldier of Muir and soldier of Ruskin shake hands.

Julia Parker works entirely outside the tradition of Muir and Ruskin. When I met her, she was sitting in her corner of Yosemite's Indian Cultural Museum, surrounded by baskets of her antecedents and teachers. She wore a red calico dress, a white crocheted shawl, necklaces of beads and shell, and a pair of old-fashioned, high-top, black leather shoes. Her legs were straight out in front of her, and the kernel of a basket was growing in her lap. The little fetal basket was exquisite. "Stop right there!" I thought. It was perfect already.

"My background is very, very lax in Indian ways," she told me. "I was born to a Pomo lady. When my mother died, I was orphaned. There were five of us in my family. We were put in a foster home, up in Santa Rosa. The lady who took us in was Mrs. Eva Williams. She wanted us to know about our Indian heritage. She'd say, 'Don't forget you're a little Indian girl.' We lived there with her for about five years, from the time I was seven to the time I was twelve. Then she found an Indian school where the five of us could be together—the Stewart Indian School near Carson City, Nevada.

"At the Indian school, they said, 'We don't want to teach Indian ways. We don't want you to learn to make baskets, or to learn your language, or anything like that, 'cause you won't need it. It'll do you more harm to do those things. This other way, you'll be able to assimilate better.'

"At the school I met my husband, Mr. Parker. After graduation he brought me over here to the park. I remember this water coming down—the waterfall. I like water. Water was coming out of this cliff, just full force, because it was May. That's when the water is really talking to you."

The water had first spoken to Mrs. Parker the same year it first spoke to me. We both arrived in Yosemite in 1947. I had been two; Mrs. Parker, seventeen. I had got lost in the valley; Mrs. Parker had begun to find herself.

"Down at the village where my husband's grandmother lived, where the Paiute and Miwok people lived, I didn't know if I wanted to be here or not. Because here they are still doing Indian ways, and I shouldn't do Indian ways.

"I overcame that feeling when I gave birth to my first child, a little girl. When the grandmother, Lucy, made a baby basket and gave it to me, I thought, 'I don't know if I want to carry my baby in this basket. People are going to make fun of me.' But Grandmother brought the basket over. It had a little design on it, a little girl design, a zigzag design. She took the baby, wrapped her up in a nice soft blanket and tied her in there. I didn't realize what it was. I just figured she was a kind lady to make that beautiful basket for me. What I realize now is it's a treasure. It's a treasure, what she did for me then.

"And my daughter liked it. I carried her around in there." Mrs. Parker looked up from her weaving and nodded at the wall. "Just behind you is an old basket that belongs to my husband's family. It's over 60 years old. My daughter graduated from her first basket into that one. It held my husband. His brothers rode in it. Then my children rode in it, then my grandchildren rode in it, and then cousins by the dozens would all want to borrow it. I let them use it."

The cradleboard was propped against the wall above Mrs. Parker's bucket of sedges, her coils of fiber. It had a wicker visor or awning to keep sun out of the baby's eyes. From the awning's edge, to entertain their babies, several generations of Indian mothers had dangled abalone shell. A flower pattern decorated the headboard. The flower was a recurrent motif in the work of the maker, the great weaver Lucy Telles—Grandma Lucy—who preceded Mrs. Parker as demonstration weaver at the Yosemite Museum.

*W*eaving chose Julia Parker, threw its warp and woof around her, as much as Julia chose weaving. In Yosemite she came to respect the old ways. She wandered under the black oaks, collecting acorns with Grandma Lucy; she watched the older woman pound them, leach them, then boil the mush with hot rocks in cooking baskets. She became friends with five of Grandma Lucy's nieces, all weavers, among them Carrie Bethel, who would become her teacher. When her husband went hunting on the east side of the Sierra, Julia went along to visit the Miwok and Paiute women there. She was always drawn to the older women's houses.

In 1955, when Grandma Lucy died, the chief naturalist in Yosemite, Doug Hubbard, suggested to Julia that she take Lucy's place. Julia declined. She was Pomo, she pointed out. It would be better to find someone indigenous to Yosemite. "So I went around and looked," she says, "and all the girls at that time had married and left.

"I went over to the east side of the Sierra, and I saw Mrs. Bethel, and I saw Mrs. Mike and Mrs. Charlie. I said, 'Would you ladies like to come over there and take Grandma Lucy's place?' They said no. They asked, 'Why don't you do it, Julia?' I said, 'I don't know how to make a basket.' So Mrs. Bethel sat down and showed me how to make a basket. She told me it was willow. She says, 'Now when you make that first basket, when you finish it, you have to give it away, Julia. You don't keep it.' I said, 'Well no one wants this crooked basket.'

She says, 'But you still must give it away.' So I followed that rule. I gave it away."

In 1960 Julia became the demonstration weaver at the Yosemite Museum. At first she used fiber gathered and prepared by the older women, then she learned how and where to find her own. Gathering the right sort of willow gave her trouble, in the beginning, until she heeded what the women said: "Willows like their feet in water." The strongest, most flexible willows were indeed those growing in water. The weavers informed her that the black in their baskets came from bracken root, and they sent her down to dig for it along the river. The bracken roots she dug were round, not flat, like the fibers her teachers had provided. She cracked the root open, and there, in the center, lay the two nice flat pieces that grow inside. Her life then was a sequence of small revelations and self-discoveries.

"Redbud, which is that red twig over there, it always kind of stumped me," she said. "Every time I used it, it would crack and break in my basket." The trick to splitting willow, a Paiute weaver showed her, was to split it out in three strips, holding one in her hand, a second in her teeth, and peeling those away from the third. That technique would not work with redbud. Julia solved redbud finally near the Merced Road, where redbud grows. The trick in splitting redbud was to lay the twig with the nodes—the little bumps from which the leaves sprout—aimed out to either side, then split the twig in half along the nodes, then peel down to the narrow width a basket weaver requires.

"It must be quite a moment," I suggested, "when you make the breakthrough and figure it out. It must be quite an emotional moment."

"Oh, yes. The plant—working with the plant. You've got to become friends with the plants."

"Do you let out a yell?"

"Well, it gets kind of emotional. Tears come in my eyes."

Tears filled Mrs. Parker's eyes at the recollection. I had guessed right about the emotion, but wrong about how it expressed itself. It was quieter and deeper than a yell. She looked away, and it was some time before she could speak.

No other weaver has mastered Julia Parker's range of aboriginal California styles. She is one of the finest living weavers of Paiute–Miwok baskets, the ultimate material expression of the culture she married into. Some years ago, she found a Pomo weaver, a woman named Mrs. McKay, who taught her the weaving of her own tribe. The Pomo, anthropologists agree, were California's consummate basket makers. Julia, now that Mrs. McKay has fallen ill, has become the master of that tradition too. She has traced her Pomo genealogy back and discovered that her great-great-grandmother was a weaver.

"When I first started collecting, I was kind of afraid to go out," Mrs. Parker told me. "Now, I just love it. I go over to the East Side, and all these willows are standing there, and the wind blows, and they're just silvery leaves, just waving to me, 'Pick me, Julia. I want to be made into a basket.'

"Every time I dream, I think about those women. I used to go on the East Side, when Lucy, and Carrie, and Minnie, and all those ladies had passed away. I would get on top of the mountain and look down and see Mono Lake—it's so pretty there. I'd drop down, and go by the houses, and I used to feel really sad that they're gone. And then my friend told me, the last teacher, my Pomo friend, she said, 'Julia, you're not alone. They're there. They're out there. You have the wind and the rain and the sun, all the animals around, you're not alone.' Now when I go to the East Side, when I'm picking willows, it sounds weird, but I can feel their presence. I feel the laughing and the singing. I hear the stories. 'You scrape the willow until it sings to you,' they said. Who'd ever think of a willow singing? But there's a certain way you scrape it, and it sings."

*J*ulia Parker had never ceased weaving as she spoke. Now, watching her fingers work, I recalled the fingers of Ansel Adams. In his old age the great photographer's hands had been arthritic. Before bad health forced him outdoors and into photography, he had trained to be a concert pianist, and the arthritis, later in life, was one of the few dirty tricks fate played on him. Even as a maestro of light and emulsion and the darkroom, he continued to play the piano beautifully, but not without a struggle against the treachery in his joints. Julia's hands were not gnarled like Ansel's, but the top joint of each finger was bent by her 30 years of weaving. Baskets get their variations in shape from variations in the pressure of the weaver's hands, she had told me. She had not mentioned that all the while the baskets are pushing back—that in the end they shape the fingers of the weaver.

I recalled the things Julia had learned from her art: The importance of good fiber in a basket. The self-discovery in weaving. The need to learn the techniques of former weavers, but never to imitate, for one's basket has to be one's own. Those rules applied in any art, I realized. I had watched Ansel Adams's hands crop Yosemite images with sheets of paper until the compositions came alive. This magic is sometimes called "inevitability," but I liked Julia's description better: "There's a certain way you scrape it, and it sings."

She and the other artists of Yosemite were working in the same tradition, after all.

Autumn tableau: Granite boulders, bathed in warm light of late afternoon, frame

an early moon and a Jeffrey pine tree at Taft Point on the rim of the valley.

"Glorious . . . are these rocks and waters arrayed in storm robes,
or chanting rejoicing in every-day dress. . . ." The waterfalls that so
elated John Muir still captivate observers. Wildcat Falls (above),
photographed at a slow shutter speed, tumbles like a cascade of
quicksilver. Spelt Creek spills like lace over a granite outcrop (right).

Winter filigrees trees and shoreline at a bend of Yosemite Valley's Merced River,

where the soft hues and clean lines of a snowy forest blend in peaceful harmony.

El Capitan glows from a field of incandescent clouds; on the southern rim rise Cathedral

Rocks. The Yosemite light show reaches a spectacular climax at sunset in the central valley.

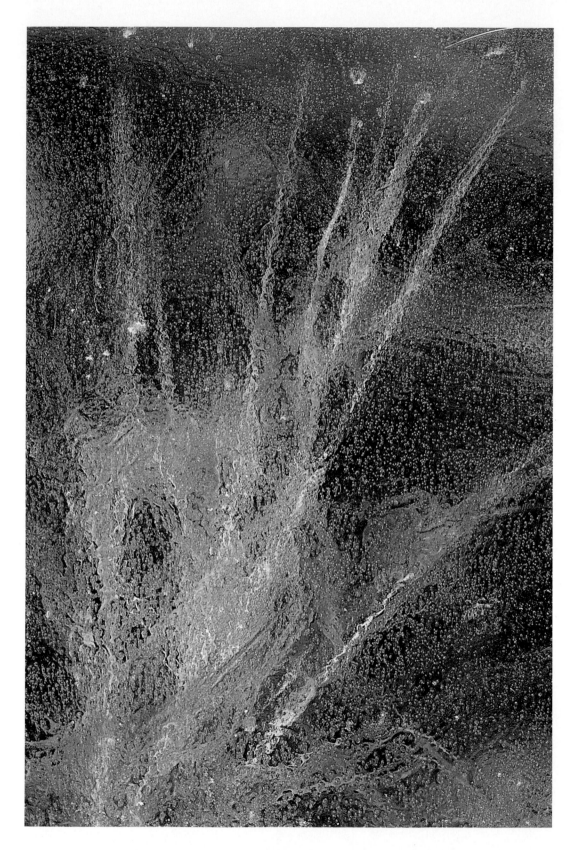

Shimmering like stained glass, grass frozen in the ice of Ostrander Lake (left) reflects a quiet beauty beyond the grandeur of cliffs and waterfalls. Poised against a granite backdrop, a trinity of black oaks with autumn leaves spread at their feet (above) imparts the elegance and tranquillity of a traditional Japanese garden.

Swept by storms that dramatize their monumental size and purity of line, El Capitan (left) and Half Dome (above) speak most tellingly of Yosemite's pull on the human spirit. "No matter how sophisticated you may be," wrote Ansel Adams, "a large granite mountain cannot be denied—it speaks in silence to the very core of your being."

The hand of man in Yosemite: Smoke rises from a prescribed burn as an October

sunset kindles the jagged peaks of Cathedral Rocks on the rim of Yosemite Valley.

Prospects: Problems and Promise

*J*im Snyder led the way through an avalanche scar, a cleanly delineated zone of bent and prostrate lodgepole pines, all pointing downhill. The avalanche had obliterated the trail, and some logging crew, cutting through the fallen ranks of trees with chain saws, had renewed it. The white circles of the cuts caught the sun like roadside reflectors. The scar ended in a stand of lodgepoles the avalanche had spared, and for a while we hiked through shade.

In the darkest shadows of the forest, Snyder's hard hat glinted silvery. He walked with a rolling, vaguely bearlike motion that had evolved, I supposed, to accommodate the jackhammers and rock bars he carried in his former career as trail builder. We emerged in a second avalanche zone, and here a spur diverged from the old trail the avalanche had ruined, detouring entirely around the scar. Snyder grunted. He was unimpressed by this bit of evasiveness and by the logging crew responsible.

"They didn't want to take the time to punch *(Continued on page 176)*

Body and mind merge into a symphony of balance and control as climber John Bachar confronts Yosemite granite. The park attracts visitors from around the world who exult in challenging nature.

171

Rafters on the Merced River drift past the two free-falling cascades of Yosemite Falls (opposite). A climber inches his way along a rope to join companions atop Lost Arrow Spire (above). That day a record 24 people gathered on the summit; the first ascent took place in 1946.
FOLLOWING PAGES: *Stone steps of Mist Trail switchback to Vernal Fall.*

it through the avalanche again—where it should have gone," Snyder said. Unnecessary ramification of trails is a cardinal sin of trail work in Jim Snyder's estimation.

In another canyon we crossed a small metal culvert in the trail. Our boots rang on the corrugated pipe. The culvert offended Snyder. He believes in building with available and natural materials. In the Sierra, that means building with rock.

Trails in the style that the English call pitching and Americans call riprap reached Yosemite in the 1870s, he told me. They came in the head of a stonemason named John Conway. "He brought the skills of rockwork to Yosemite," Snyder said. "Conway knew a tremendous amount about the country. I can't say that from anything he wrote. It's just from looking at the trails he built. The Four Mile Trail, for example. The Park Service rebuilt it in the 1920s. You look at where the Park Service put its trail, and you look where Conway put his. What Conway obviously did was climb all over the mountains and say, 'How can I get from here to there, and what obstacles do I have to avoid?' His trail is steeper and narrower. The Park Service trail has gentle gradients, big loops for views. The Park Service people were thinking about width. They had started to think of trails as roads. The Model T had come in. People began to think of wheel engineering instead of *foot* engineering.

"The Yosemite Falls Trail is the only one of Conway's that the Park Service didn't really revamp in the '20s," Snyder continued. "It's on roughly the same alignment it was in his day. Some of Conway's walls are still up there in use. The trail to Nevada Fall is the oldest trail in continuous use in the park. There's a wall there built by Conway. He didn't use any cut rock. He used what he had. His rock is laid in courses, the big stones mixed in with the small ones as he got it. The guy knew what he was doing. He wasn't just stacking rocks. He was building a wall. He was an artist. He knew the rock, and he felt it. He had a tremendous feeling for the materials of the place."

*T*wo weeks before our trip, Snyder had been invited as consultant to advise a trail crew building with riprap in nearby Stanislaus National Forest. After observing the crew for a while, he gave his opinion: "You guys are looking at the rock and making it fit your mind. You've got to do it the other way around. Make your mind fit the rock."

This was a neat encapsulation of Snyder's philosophy, and it struck me that it might serve as credo for all development in Yosemite. Snyder's trails, and the principles behind them, would make a fine model for how things should be done—but often are not—in Yosemite and all national parks.

The Wilderness Society has identified Yosemite as one of America's ten most endangered parks. The Sierra Club, the Yosemite Association, various other environmental groups, and thousands of concerned citizens are worried as well. At present, Yosemite Valley contains a small town: markets, a bank, a jail, homes, apartments, and pizza, ice cream, and beauty parlors—more than a thousand buildings in all. The valley has nearly 30 miles of roadway, a million vehicles annually, traffic jams, air pollution, juvenile delinquents, drunks. Yosemite, in other words, reflects the ills of society at large.

In the 1989 summer issue of *Wilderness,* the Wilderness Society journal, Richard Reinhardt described the end of his illusion that Yosemite was changeless. "We were wrong, of course," he wrote. "Yosemite was far from changeless. It was temporal and precarious; and its comforts, its accessible delights—the very qualities we had learned to love—were putting the Valley in terrible jeopardy. With regret and shame, I began to learn what our careless love had done."

This sort of prose has its own genre, the "Fatal Beauty" school of Yosemite writing, and it dates back at least as far as the "Yosemite's Fatal Beauty" article William Colby wrote in 1948. The language has changed little since then. For me, Yosemite is less precarious, less in jeopardy, than many of the fatalists think, but there is plenty of cause for worry. It is difficult, building a parking lot or a delicatessen, to "make your mind fit the rock," as Jim Snyder teaches.

"I think dynamite has become a substitute for good work and hard work in a lot of forests and parks," he told me in the backcountry. "It's too easy, and nobody thinks about the future consequences of using it. We never think about what happened half a century ago, or what will happen a century hence."

My attention shifted to the dents and dings on Jim Snyder's hard hat. They had come, I supposed, from fly rock—granite "shrapnel" from explosions. Snyder is not fond of explosives, and in his former career he avoided their use whenever possible, yet for many years he was one of Yosemite's expert blasters. Occasionally, he is still called upon to "shoot" granite.

"After the First World War, dynamite came in," he went on. "You could get it surplus for almost nothing. You could get it free from the Army. Trail builders started using dynamite as a substitute for skilled labor. After the war, they put trails where they'd never been before in Yosemite. One of them is up the Merced River. It's just blown out of the rock. It's a powder exercise. It causes us no end of maintenance problems, because there's not a rock left that hasn't been blown to shreds. There's nothing there to work with."

I have seen this stretch of trail above the Merced. It switchbacks up the rock, as white and ugly as the scar on Ahab's face.

The ultimate powder exercise in Yosemite National Park—the Alamogordo and Hiroshima of powder exercises—resulted in the Tioga Road just west of Tenaya Lake. I can think of no better example, anywhere on the planet, of where and how *not* to build a road.

Tenaya Lake is bordered by some of the finest glacier-polished rock on earth. When Tenaya, the old chief of the Yosemites, was informed that the lake had been named after him, he replied sourly that it already had a name, and a perfectly good one: *Pywiack,* "Lake of the Shining Rocks." Lake of the Shining Rocks it is. Northwest of that glittery lakeshore, the rounded terrain is breached by a particularly wide and beautiful slope of granite. Its curve emerges huge, pale, and gibbous from the pines. It is as if the moon, miscalculating its orbit, had tried to rise in the middle of Yosemite. Great patches of the rock, buffed to a high shine by the glaciers, glare in the sun.

In the late 1950s, a new route for the old Tioga Road was surveyed straight across the middle of this granite, its path marked by small yellow flags. My little brother and I walked the flagged course with my father, who was then executive director of the Sierra Club and was waging a campaign against the rerouted road. My brother and I were serving, as we often did in those days, as models— human figures to show the scale of the country in propaganda photographs my father took. I assumed that this time my father would win. I thought it would be evident to everyone. This was Yosemite National Park! As soon as my father informed the public, the public would put a stop to the new road.

Trailing him, my brother and I began pulling out survey flags. Today environmental vigilantes call this "desurveying," but we had no name for it—hardly even thought about it. It just seemed the natural thing to do. It was also illegal, and when my father saw what we were up to, he told us to stop. My father lost the campaign. The new road was built, a deep bench-cut blasted straight through the shining landscape. The roadbed is supported on the downhill side by a fill of crushed granite and boulders. The scar is visible, I imagine, from high orbit.

I can't drive that road today without remembering specific logs I stepped over in walking this route; without remembering certain flags I desurveyed. Each time I round the corner and start across that mutilated slope, there comes a heartsickness at what was lost and a black anger at the perpetrators. We can never allow another errant road like that one in Yosemite.

Another madness of the 1950s was the National Park Service campaign against a moth—the lodgepole needle-miner. The needle-miner larva periodically defoliates expanses of Yosemite's lodgepole forest. The moth is not an exotic pest, but indigenous. Moth and lodgepole are old acquaintances; a lodgepole can suffer about seven attacks by the needle-miner before it dies; and yet park managers throughout Yosemite's history have fought the moth tooth and nail. In the old days, they followed a scorched-earth policy, cutting and burning infested trees and zones of healthy trees around. The 1913 campaign was literally a cavalry exercise, for the U.S. Cavalry then ran the park. In the 1950s, the Park Service sprayed DDT. The pesticide had little long-term effect on the moth but was devastating to other Yosemite wildlife. What I remember of that time is the corpses of birds alongside the Tioga Road. DDT in high concentrations was showing up in Yosemite's streams.

In the middle of the 1950s, as the 50th anniversary of the National Park Service approached, there was much discussion—as with the approach of Yosemite's centennial—of undermaintenance and disrepair in national parks. Instead of simply correcting problems of undermaintenance, the Park Service launched a ten-year program of new construction that was called "Mission 66." Infrastructure bloomed, little of it guided by the sensible principles that came down to us from John Conway through intermediaries like Jim Snyder.

In the last two decades, one big management enterprise in Yosemite has been "prescribed burning" of forests. Almost everyone believes these fires are a good thing. There is a sort of natural imperative to it. Its purpose is to correct past mismanagement—to eliminate understory fuel accumulated through a half-century of misguided and unnatural fire suppression. But the day should come, it seems to me, when all that unnatural fuel is consumed and the forest reverts to a seminatural state, thereafter left to burn on its own schedule. I have yet to meet a prescribed burner whose eyes are fixed on that great day.

*W*e need to protect our parks from management dogma, and we need to keep good ideas from becoming dogma. More than anything, we need to protect our parks from human whim. Yosemite's managers should devote their energies to managing humans in the park. The ecosystem of Yosemite should be left to manage itself.

The General Management Plan for Yosemite was released by the Park Service in 1980. Thousands of citizens who care about Yosemite, in 48 public workshops around the nation, contributed their ideas. The plan calls for removing all automobiles from the valley and from Mariposa Grove and for

179

redirecting development in the valley to the park's periphery. Park Service administration buildings would be moved to El Portal. Shuttles would carry visitors into the valley from outlying parking facilities. In its general intent, the plan is sound. There are small practical problems with certain details— insufficient room at El Portal, for example, and the dependence of the great gray owl on meadows where parking facilities would be expanded. There are big problems with funding. The plan is being altered and will be delayed. These are setbacks, yet Yosemite faces no imminent calamity.

*T*hose gloomiest about Yosemite, I have noticed, are usually those with the shortest acquaintance with the place. They come often with unrealistic expectations. It is foolish to compare Yosemite with Ahwahnee, the valley the Indians knew. Yosemite Valley has not been wilderness for 140 years. The first tourist arrived four years after the Mariposa Battalion entered the valley, and tourists have swarmed the place since. "The tide of visitors will float slowly about the *bottom* of the valley . . . leaving the rocks and falls eloquent as ever and instinct with imperishable beauty and greatness," John Muir wrote, and it's true. It is still possible—easy, except on big holidays—to find places to be alone with the valley. If crowds are anathema to you, don't go to Yosemite on Memorial Day.

There have always been complaints about Yosemite's throngs, and there always will be. Today's visitors complain about pollution from car exhausts; my grandmother complained about dust from stagecoaches. If there were more than five families camped in the valley, it felt crowded, she used to tell us.

Old-timers, I have noticed, tend to be more sanguine about the valley's prospects. Ansel Adams, for example, was much less troubled by conditions in Yosemite than the average cameraman doing a television news special in the Fatal Beauty style. My father, another old Yosemite hand, is impressed, rather than appalled, by how the park handles its numbers. It helps to have some perspective; my father has more than 70 years of it. When he first came in 1918, at the age of six, 35,500 people visited the park annually. One hundred times that many visit today. He still finds Yosemite one of the wonders of the earth and comes whenever he can. In 1937, when my father worked in Yosemite, half a million visited annually. Although 3.5 million visit today, he testifies that there are few—if any—more buildings in the valley than there were when he lived there. And I can still spend an uncrowded afternoon walking the perimeter of the valley. Despite problems, the message of Yosemite National Park, after a hundred years, is not how badly the park is run but how well.

By the end of this century, the last of the world's wildernesses will have been spoken for: preserved, if they are going to be, compromised if not. The challenge of the next centuries on this planet—inside Yosemite and other planetary parks, as well as outside—will be restoration of degraded country. The return of the peregrine falcon to the park and the reintroduction of the bighorn sheep in Yosemite are promising beginnings.

The wild sheep, or bighorn, John Muir believed, was the finest animal mountaineer in the high country. Muir and the sheep shared a habitat preference. The bighorn was one of his favorite animals.

"Possessed of keen sight and scent, and strong limbs, he dwells secure amid the loftiest summits, leaping unscathed from crag to crag, up and down the fronts of giddy precipices, crossing foaming torrents and slopes of frozen snow, exposed to the wildest storms, yet maintaining a brave, warm life, and developing from generation to generation in perfect strength and beauty."

The sheep, Muir thought, was safe in its mountain fastness. "Man is the most dangerous enemy of all, but even from him our brave mountain-dweller has little to fear in the remote solitudes of the High Sierra." This time Muir was wrong. The wild sheep's instinctive defense—standing perfectly motionless on some ridge or crag—works fine against mountain lions but not against rifles. In 1883 the California legislature acted to protect the species, but the law did little good. Decimated by the meat-hunting of miners, pressured by competitive grazing of domestic sheep, weakened by domestic-sheep diseases, wild sheep virtually disappeared from Yosemite by the turn of the century.

It is an old story, repeated endlessly in the taming of wild country. And yet recently it received a new twist. In March 1986, after an absence of generations, sheep from a southern Sierra herd were reintroduced to the east side of Yosemite. For the past two years, Les Chow, a graduate student at the University of California, has been monitoring the released sheep. Chow has been observing their movements both by spotting scope and by radio (a number of the adults are fitted with radio collars). He has been following on foot, mostly, but also by air. The day before one of his telemetry flights, he filled me in on his work and his subjects.

"We're interested, among other things, in how they go about exploring and settling new terrain," he said. "How are patterns of home range established? Sheep are very conservative in their exploration. Their ecology and their evolution have combined to restrict them to little islands of habitat. They require particular things. They want to be very close to escape terrain, for example—terrain extremely broken and rough. Ewes with lambs are the most conservative of all, especially when the lambs are young. The rams are more adventurous. In 1988, one ram walked all the way to Tuolumne Meadows and stood on top of Lembert Dome.

"Bighorns, between the ears, don't look like they have very much going on," Chow continued. "But they're good at doing what they do. They go from Point A to Point B unerringly. They are interesting behaviorally, but their behaviors are subtle. We pick a sheep at random and watch it forage in one spot for ten minutes. What is the distance to escape terrain? What is the substrate in that spot? What are the plants? Sheep wander all over to eat, but we've found that the places they return to repeatedly are little wet meadows and seeps."

At the end of each summer pursuing sheep, Chow and his colleague, Peggy Moore, are nearly as fit as their subjects. Their rhythms, their haunts, their views—their *lives*—are essentially the lives of sheep.

"The days are really long," Chow said, searching for words. "But it's beautiful country. We've learned an awful lot about alpine plants. It takes getting down on your knees and pressing your nose to the ground to find out what the sheep have been nipping off. Sheep fill up once when they're born, then spend the rest of their lives walking around and topping off. Eat a flower here. Two or three blades from this clump. Move on to something else."

To date, 38 sheep have been released at the boundary of the park, and the population now stands at 41. The birthrate has crept past the death rate. The reintroduction has been a modest success.

Waiting in Yosemite National Park, under water, is a potential masterpiece of restoration, the recovery project to end all recovery projects; an enterprise which, if realized, would become a paradigm for all planetary restoration to come. Yosemite has a twin. When the block of the Sierra rose and tilted west, and its westward-flowing streams carved their courses deeper, and those stream courses were then excavated by glacial ice, it happened not just in one place, but all along the range.

For John Muir, these ice-carved valleys were all "yosemites." The Yosemite we know was only the finest of them. On the Tuolumne River is a valley named Hetch Hetchy. "A wonderfully exact counterpart of the Merced Yosemite," Muir wrote. His language was echoed in the no-nonsense report of California state geologist Josiah Whitney in 1868. Whitney noted that Hetch Hetchy wasn't quite so grand, but recommended it to travelers, "if it be only to see how curiously nature has repeated herself."

The city of San Francisco, after a long political battle with Muir and his Sierra Club, built a dam in the Hetch Hetchy Valley of the Tuolumne. For water and hydroelectric power San Francisco drowned Yosemite's twin. The fight against the dam, and its invasion of Yosemite National Park, was John Muir's last fight. My father, along with many other people, believes that the loss of

Hetch Hetchy "might have instilled the huge grief that hastened his death."

From infancy, I think, I have heard my father dream aloud of a day when the dam in Hetch Hetchy might be removed. In the last days of the Reagan Administration, the suggestion was repeated by outgoing Secretary of the Interior Donald Hodel. We should do it. We are confronted, in the restoration of Yosemite, with nearly insurmountable opportunities.

*T*he winter before Yosemite's centennial, my parents and I paused in the parking lot at Yosemite Village and looked up. We were not far from the spot where, at the age of two, I had disappeared to explore the valley on my own. My father was studying his old climbing routes, I supposed, but I was wrong. He nodded up at Glacier Point. "I wonder when the scar of the firefall will recover," he said.

The firefall was an old Yosemite tradition. Every night in the summer, a bonfire of red-fir bark was built on Glacier Point. From Camp Curry below came the cry, "Let the fire fall!" And down it poured, a slender cataract of lava splitting the dark cliff. It was a bad idea, probably—no current management plan calls for a rekindling of the firefall—but it certainly was spectacular. There have been no firefalls since 1968, yet a pale scar still shows where the fire burned away the cliff's lichens. Lichens are one of my father's interests. The recovery of damaged landscapes is another of them.

While my parents and I gazed up, a balding, fiftyish man in a red pile jacket started across the parking lot, then detoured toward us. He saw a tall, white-haired man and a woman in their late seventies and their middle-aged son. He seemed to have mistaken our ruminations for perplexity. He approached us. "Do you folks know what you're looking at?" he asked helpfully.

"Yes," my father said.

Pointing to the granite prominences above us, he began calling out the names. "Paiute Point. Lost Arrow. Yosemite Point. Yosemite Point Couloir. . . ."

Yosemite Point Couloir, it happens, was one of my father's first ascents. Without turning, he began identifying features behind him, pointing unerringly to peaks and prominences he could not see. They were permanent features of an interior landscape.

"Excuse me," the man said, and he retreated, smiling.

The little incident started a train of thought. My father can be a show-off. Muir often showed off, too. It is by now a cliché of dozens of journalists writing features in Sunday supplements, but Muir and my father really are very much alike. There are disparities, of course, but also a remarkable number of convergences between these two men for whom Yosemite was central.

Yosemite once had an official guardian, a man committed to the place. The first man to hold the position was Galen Clark. For Yosemite's prospects to remain bright, it seems to me, the park will need more guardians. Good management plans, wise policies, won't be enough. Yosemite needs a few strong individuals. It needs advocates, men and women for whom Yosemite is not just a career, but a mission—people like Galen Clark and John Muir and David Brower. I worry sometimes that in the new generations we are lacking the necessary fire and eccentricity.

Lately I have been keeping an eye on my son. He is four and, like his grandfather, is named David Brower.

The new David Brower has fine balance and is a natural climber. Recently, at his grandparents' house, he disappeared while we were watching a television documentary on his namesake. The documentary had been intercut with some old, flickery movie footage of his grandfather rock-climbing, and it was in the middle of this that my son vanished. We found him in the backyard, climbing a difficult pitch on an incense cedar transplanted from the Sierra by the older David Brower 40 years before. The younger David Brower had wrapped a dog leash around his waist for a rope, and he was halfway up.

The new David Brower loves Yosemite, especially the waterfalls, and often asks when we are going back. This is hardly surprising, I suppose. He has five generations of involvement with the place in his genes.

Recently, in the Four Seasons Restaurant on the Yosemite Valley floor, my son and I were awaiting our food when John Muir walked in. He had just finished a lecture—"Stickeen and Other Fellow Mortals; Another Evening with John Muir"—and had come in for a bite. This Muir was the incarnation named Lee Stetson, an actor who for a number of years has played the old conservationist in one-man shows. My son and Muir, who had never met, detected one another's auras and played eye games across the crowded room. Muir peeked from behind his scraggly prophet's beard, my son from underneath the table.

The next afternoon found us walking down the trail from the biggest of the giant sequoias of the Mariposa Grove, at Yosemite's southern border. We had just seen the Grizzly Giant, the California Tunnel Tree, the Galen Clark Tree, the Faithful Couple. My son was riding on my shoulders.

I was feeling chastened, as usual, by the age, the patience, the colossal cathedral quiet of the Big Trees. My son was mostly tired. He had begun the walk throwing sequoia cones about, then had turned to collecting them. I had read him the admonition in the trail guide: "Please remember to leave all cones where you find them for other visitors to enjoy." We couldn't take the cones home, I explained, for then they would never grow into giant sequoias. He understood instantly and dumped his collection.

A prescribed burn was being conducted some miles away. Giant sequoias depend on fire for their regeneration, and the burn was searing away the duff to allow for that. The scene had subtly shifted red, as happens when the sun shines through smoke. The giant sequoias were bathed in a slightly muted, vaguely tannic light. It made for an odd sensation. It was like walking through a memory. It was like wandering in some former age when atmospheric gases were in different balance—the Age of Dinosaurs, perhaps, where these gigantic trees belonged.

*W*e overtook two silver-haired women in their mid-60s. As we came up behind, one of them picked up a sequoia cone. She rolled it in her hand as she walked, then casually—furtively—slipped it into her pocket.

"Dad!" my son said. "She put that pinecone in her pocket!"

"Well . . ." I said.

"She's not s'posed to take it!"

"Well, there are lots of other cones, Davey."

I winced at my own equivocation. Sometimes true mettle in these matters skips generations. Two paces behind the poor woman, we discussed the cone she had stolen, Davey loudly, I as quietly and soothingly as I could. Davey seemed to be under the impression that the cone might grow into a sequoia in her pocket. This would have been an excruciatingly slow and hideous death, all right. I assured him the danger was small. There came a moment of peace, and I thought I had mollified this David Brower.

"But she put it in her pocket," he said.

I swung wide around the women and passed. I felt Davey twist on my shoulders—to glare back, I suppose, at the cone-stealer. Yosemite, I decided, might have its new guardians after all.

185

Campfire radiates a circle of warmth at Lower River Campground. With summer

crowds gone, winter offers tranquillity—an increasingly elusive quality in Yosemite.

*Snow mantles the valley's north rim beyond the rustic architecture
of the Ahwahnee Hotel. Built in 1927 of local stone and timber,
it offers visitors an elegant—if expensive—alternative to crowded
campsites. Above, an instructor teaches cross-country students
at California's oldest ski resort, Badger Pass, established in 1935.*

Visitors learn about the history of Yosemite, its plants and animals, and the impact

of people on the park during a summer nature walk led by ranger Bob Clarillos.

Queuing up at the entrance, hopefuls wait for a vacancy at one of 18
campgrounds in Yosemite. The National Park Service limits the number of
campers to prevent overcrowding and to enhance each person's experience.
At left, shafts of morning sunlight brush Upper River Campground.
FOLLOWING PAGES: A hang glider soars in solitary freedom above the mist-
strewn valley. With careful management, century-old Yosemite National
Park can continue to provide a magnificent sanctuary for the human spirit.

Illustrations Credits

FRONT MATTER—1 James Randklev; 2-3 Jeff Grandy; 4-5 Dewitt Jones; 7 ©Barbara Brundege/Eugene Fisher; 8 ©Ed Cooper.

MY YOSEMITE—10 Galen Rowell/Mountain Light; 15 Adapted from a map by the U.S. Geological Survey; 16-17 Adapted from a map by Pali Arts Communications/American Park Network, San Francisco, CA.

FIRE AND ICE—18 ©Pat O'Hara; 20 William Neill; 21 R. L. Patterson; 22-23 William Neill; 30 Galen Rowell/Mountain Light; 31 William Neill; 32-33 Dewitt Jones; 34 ©Carr Clifton/ALLSTOCK; 35 Dewitt Jones; 36-37 ©Pat O'Hara; 38-39 ©David Muench, 1990.

MAN IN THE PARK—40 Studebaker Corporation of America; 42 Yosemite Research Library—NPS; 43 (both) R. L. Patterson; 44-45 Yosemite Research Library—NPS; 56-57 Courtesy of the Bancroft Library; 58 J. T. Boysen; 59 (upper) Yosemite Research Library—NPS; 59 (lower) Southern Pacific Railroad Company; 60 Photograph by Francis M. Fultz, Courtesy of the Muir-Hanna Trust, University of the Pacific Libraries; 61 (upper) Yosemite Research Library—NPS; 61 (lower) ©Barbara Brundege/Eugene Fisher.

THE LIVING PARK—62 William Neill; 64 ©Pat O'Hara; 65 ©Carr Clifton; 66-67 Charles Cramer; 78-80 William Neill; 81 Jeff Grandy; 82-83 Dewitt Jones; 84 Jay Dickman; 85 Galen Rowell/Mountain Light; 86-87 Charles Cramer; 88-89 Jeff Nicholas; 90-91 William Neill; 92-93 Michael Frye; 94 Howard Weamer; 95 Michael Frye; 96, 97 (upper, lower right) Howard Weamer; 97 (lower left) ©Ed Cooper; 98-99 Michael Frye.

THE HIGH COUNTRY—100 Galen Rowell/Mountain Light; 102 Howard Weamer; 103 ©Pat O'Hara; 104-105 ©Carr Clifton; 116-117 Larry Ulrich; 118 Dewitt Jones; 119 ©Carr Clifton; 120-121 Dewitt Jones; 122-125 Howard Weamer; 126-127 Michael Frye; 128-129 Howard Weamer; 130 Chip Carroon/ALLSTOCK; 131 ©Carr Clifton/ALLSTOCK; 132-133 Galen Rowell/Mountain Light.

VALLEY OF THE RANGE OF LIGHT—134 Yosemite Research Library—NPS; 136 Courtesy of the Center For Creative Photography; 137 (upper) Jay Dickman; 137 (lower left) ©Barbara Brundege/Eugene Fisher; 137 (lower right) Yosemite Research Library—NPS; 138-139 Haggin Collection, The Haggin Museum, Stockton, CA; 144 Photograph by Ansel Adams, Courtesy of The Trustees of The Ansel Adams Publishing Rights Trust, All Rights Reserved; 145 Ted Orland; 146-149 Photographs by Ansel Adams, Courtesy of The Trustees of The Ansel Adams Publishing Rights Trust, All Rights Reserved; 156-157 ©Pat O'Hara; 158 Jeff Nicholas; 159 Howard Weamer; 160-161 William Neill; 162-163 Keith Stewart Walklet; 164 Howard Weamer; 165 ©Carr Clifton; 166 James Peter Stuart/ALLSTOCK; 167 Tom Meyers; 168-169 Jeff Grandy.

PROSPECTS: PROBLEMS AND PROMISE—170 Galen Rowell/Mountain Light; 172 ©Harald Sund; 173 Lewis Kemper; 174-175 Lewis Kemper/DRK PHOTO; 186-187 Dewitt Jones; 188 John Poimiroo; 189 Robert Holmes; 190-193 Jay Dickman; 194-95 Bill Ross/WESTLIGHT.

BACK MATTER—198 Michael Frye.

Acknowledgments

The Special Publications Division is grateful to the individuals, groups, and organizations named and quoted in the text and to those cited here for their generous assistance during the preparation of this book.

YOSEMITE NATIONAL PARK: Craig D. Bates, Curator of Ethnography; Scott Carpenter, Park Archaeologist; Lisa Dapprich, Public Affairs Officer; Linda Eade, Research Librarian; Donald Fox, Park Landscape Architect; and Mallory Smith, Public Affairs Assistant.

SMITHSONIAN INSTITUTION: Dave Bohaska, Robert K. Emry, and Clayton E. Ray of the Department of Paleobiology, Museum of Natural History.

U.S. GEOLOGICAL SURVEY: N. King Huber, Jim Pinkerton, William V. Sliter, and Richard S. Williams, Jr.

We also thank the following for sharing their experience and expertise with us: R. Scott Anderson, Bilby Research Center, Northern Arizona University; Terry M. Mansfield, California Department of Fish and Game; John Poimiroo, Yosemite Park and Curry Co.; Bob Roney; The Yosemite Fund.

Additional Reading

The reader may wish to consult the *National Geographic* index for related articles and books. Of particular interest are the following: David S. Boyer, "Yosemite—Forever?", NATIONAL GEOGRAPHIC, January 1985, and Edwin Kiester, Jr., "Winter in Yosemite," NATIONAL GEOGRAPHIC TRAVELER, Winter 1988-89.

The following books may be of special interest: Ansel Adams, *Ansel Adams: An Autobiography*; Ansel Adams and Nancy Newhall, *This is the American Earth*; Doris Ostrander Dawdy, *Artists of the American West*; Joseph Grinnell and Tracy Irwin Storer, *Animal Life in the Yosemite*; Robert F. Heizer (ed.) and the Smithsonian Institution, *Handbook of North American Indians: Vol. 8, California*; N. King Huber, *The Geologic Story of Yosemite National Park*; Clarence King, *Mountaineering in the Sierra Nevada*; John Muir, *The Yosemite*; John Muir, *The Mountains of California*; Donald Culross Peattie, *A Natural History of Western Trees*; Margaret Sanborn, *Yosemite: Its Discovery, Its Wonders and Its People*; Shirley Sargent, *Yosemite & Its Innkeepers* and *Yosemite: The First 100 Years—1890-1990*; Lowell Sumner and Joseph S. Dixon, *Birds and Mammals of the Sierra Nevada*; Michael D. Yandell, *National Parkways: A Photographic and Comprehensive Guide to Yosemite National Park*.

Composition by the Typographic section of National Geographic Production Services, Pre-Press Division. Printed and bound by R. R. Donnelley & Sons, Willard, Ohio. Color separations by Graphic Art Service, Inc., Nashville, Tenn.; Lanman Progressive Co., Washington, D.C.; Lincoln Graphics, Inc., Cherry Hill, N.J.; and NEC, Inc., Nashville, Tenn. Dust jacket printed by Federated Lithographers-Printers, Inc., Providence, R.I.

Index

Boldface indicates illustrations; *italic* refers to picture captions.

BLACK BEAR'S SIGNATURE: ADULTS BLAZE
TRAILSIDE TREES WITH CLAWS OR TEETH.

198

Library of Congress CIP Data
Brower, Kenneth, 1944-
    Yosemite: an American treasure / by Kenneth Brower: prepared by the Special Publications Division, National Geographic Society.
        p.   cm.
    Includes bibliographical references
    ISBN 0-87044-789-0
    ISBN 0-87044-794-7 (lib. bdg.)
        1. Yosemite National Park (Calif.) I. National Geographic Society (U.S.). Special Publications Division. II. Title.
F868.Y6B827   1990
917.94'47—dc20   90-5655
                                                                          CIP

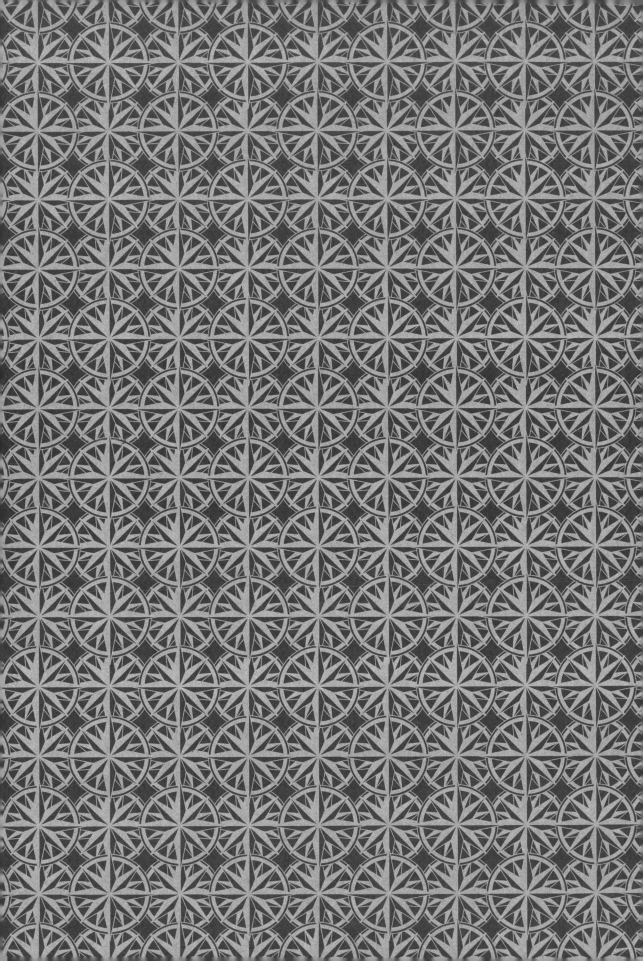